Basic KAYAKING

All the Skills and Gear You Need to Get Started

Wayne Dickert,
paddling consultant

Jon Rounds, editor

Photographs by Skip Brown

Illustrations by Roberto Sabas

STACKPOLE BOOKS

0   11557 03210   9

Published by
STACKPOLE BOOKS
5067 Ritter Road
Mechanicsburg, PA 17055
www.stackpolebooks.com

Printed in China

10 9 8 7 6 5 4 3 2 1

First edition

Cover design by Tracy Patterson

Illustrations by Roberto Sabas

All photographs by Skip Brown except as follows:
Alan Wycheck: 6–11; Pat McDonnell: 17 (water launch), 72–73;
Watermark: 1, 4–5.

Library of Congress Cataloging-in-Publication Data

Basic kayaking : all the skills and gear you need to get
started / Jon Rounds, editor ; Wayne Dickert, paddling
consultant ; photographs by Skip Brown ; illustrations by
Roberto Sabas.— 1st ed.
        p. cm.
 ISBN 0-8117-3210-X
 1. Kayaking. I. Rounds, Jon. II. Brown, Skip, 1957– III. Sabas,
Roberto.
GV783.B377 2005
797.122'4—dc22

                                        2005002370

 ISBN 978-0-8117-3210-9

Contents

Acknowledgments

Wayne Dickert, head of instruction at Nantahala Outdoor Center in Bryson City, North Carolina, is the expert behind this book. An Olympic paddler and long-time whitewater paddling instructor, "Wayner" is not only an expert boater but a veteran teacher. He directed this book, from outline to final revision, and did all the paddling for the photos.

Skip Brown, perhaps the most-published photographer of paddlesports in the business (for good reason) and an expert kayaker himself, did whatever was necessary, as usual, to deliver the shots we needed.

Likewise, we all appreciated the patient, skillful work of illustrator Roberto Sabas.

Thanks go to Matt Porter of Watermark for providing images of Dagger kayaks.

Many thanks to Mary Liskow and Doug Gibson of Blue Mountain Outfitters in Marysville, Pennsylvania, on the Susquehanna River, for loaning us equipment to photograph and taking the time to explain its use. Today's boater is confronted with a baffling array of boats, paddles, clothing, and accessories, and Blue Mountain has not only a vast selection but the expertise to guide you toward the right choices for your particular needs. In fact, one generalization about equipment became abundantly clear to me while working on this book: Buy it at a paddling shop. You'll be dealing with real people who are paddlers themselves and, unlike shopping on-line or through the mail, you'll be able to pick up the paddle, try on the clothes, and compare the models, styles, and sizes.

Finally, thanks to all the good folks at Stackpole Books, in particular Judith Schnell, Mark Allison, Chris Chappell, and Caroline Stover, who made working on this book a pleasure.

—Jon Rounds

Introduction

Kayaking may be the most fun you can have in a boat. No craft is as responsive to a paddle stroke as a kayak, and none is better suited to navigating fast water. You wear the boat, your every move translated into an immediate reaction, and once you know how to control it and understand the dynamics of the river, getting out on the water is a real thrill. The kayaks themselves have evolved from their origins as Arctic hunting craft into a vast array of styles, ranging from the stubby rodeo boats used in freestyle competitions to the sleek touring kayaks built for distance paddling on the ocean. In between are kayaks for every size and skill level of paddler.

Many introductory kayaking books provide an overview of the entire world of kayaking, with brief sections on whitewater, touring, and recreational equipment and a few basic skills specific to each style. This book is designed specifically for the beginner who wants clear, graphic instruction on the basics of whitewater kayaking, from choosing and outfitting a boat to learning the essential strokes, braces, rolls, and river moves. The skills involved fall into two categories. First are the basic boat-handling skills of balancing and leaning a boat, followed by the fundamental techniques you need to be able to move around. Second are the on-the-water skills of reading the river and doing the moves—eddy turns, peel-outs, and ferries—that get you from place to place.

We have taken nothing for granted. We show every step of every technique, from putting on a spray skirt to doing the Eskimo roll. Our goal is to provide the most clear and thorough instruction on the essential skills of whitewater kayaking.

1

Gearing Up

KAYAKS

The three main types of kayaks on the market today are whitewater, recreational, and touring (or sea) kayaks. Whitewater kayaks are the shortest and most maneuverable of the three. Many varieties and specialized designs are on the market today. Descriptions later in this chapter will help you choose the boat that best suits your needs.

Recreational kayaks range from about $9^1/_2$ to 14 feet and are a little wider and more stable than touring kayaks. They're suited for paddling on lakes or gentle rivers, and because of their width, stability, and storage space, they make good boats for fishing, photography, or sightseeing.

Touring or sea kayaks range from 14 to 17 feet and are designed for the serious long-distance paddler. Long and sleek, they are built for speed on lakes, rivers without difficult rapids, or the ocean. The lightest and most expensive models are made of high-tech materials, such as Kevlar.

Neither recreational nor touring kayaks are suited for whitewater beyond Class II. (See pages 78–79 for an explanation of river classification.)

Whitewater kayaks, like the Kingpin, by Dagger, are shorter and more maneuverable than recreational or touring kayaks.

Recreational kayaks are longer than whitewater boats, are very stable, and hold a lot of gear, but they are not very maneuverable and not suitable for running whitewater.

Touring kayaks (sea kayaks) like the Dagger Charleston are built for long trips on lakes or the ocean, but are not suitable for whitewater. They have the longest hulls of the three kayak types.

Note the difference in length and shape between a touring kayak (left) and a whitewater boat.

KAYAK DESIGN ELEMENTS

The body of a kayak is referred to as the hull. Before shopping for any type of kayak, it helps to understand the basic features of hull design that can tell you at a glance a boat's strengths and weaknesses.

Length. In general, the shorter the boat, the easier it turns but the slower it moves when going in a straight line. Thus, boats designed for doing freestyle tricks, such as squirt boats and rodeo boats, tend to be the shortest of all kayaks, some of them under 6 feet. By contrast, a longer boat "tracks" better—it stays on course, with less veering during forward strokes—and also has more hull speed. Thus, downriver boats are long, from $8^{1}/_{2}$ to 10 feet. A good length for an all-around whitewater kayak is somewhere between 7 and 9 feet, depending on your size.

Volume. The volume of a kayak is expressed by the number of gallons it will hold. Obviously, a longer, wider, deeper boat has more volume, but the more significant design issue is how the volume is distributed. You will notice that playboats designed for surfing waves and doing tricks have thin snouts and tails that make the boat easy to spin and to put into dives for vertical moves like cartwheels and "enders" as well as "mystery moves"—tricks done underwater. All the volume in such boats is concentrated in the middle, around the cockpit. These features make radical freestyle boats hard to control, especially for beginners.

The exact opposite of this design is the creek boat, a high-volume kayak that is thick and rounded from bow to stern, designed to ride high and surface quickly after the steep drops of severe whitewater runs.

Shape of Bottom. The flatter the bottom of the boat is from one side to the other, the more freely it will turn, but the less well it will track. A flat hull is called a planing hull, because the boat rides high on the water, literally skidding across the surface, and so is very easy to maneuver back and forth with quick paddle strokes. The opposite of a planing hull is a displacement hull, which is more rounded, sits deeper in the water, and tracks better. It also has more hull speed.

A displacement hull (top) curves smoothly from bow to stern and from side to side, a design that cause it to sit lower in the water than a planing hull (bottom), which is flat where it contacts the water.

2

Pronounced rocker (whitewater playboat)

Rocker. Rocker is the amount of curvature along the bottom of a hull from bow to stern. A boat with pronounced rocker turns very quickly because its bow and stern are raised and the boat is pivoting on a very short length of hull. This short hull also makes for a slower boat. Freestyle and creek boats have pronounced rocker, for tricks and general maneuverability; all-around whitewater kayaks have mild rocker; and downriver and touring boats have nearly flat bottoms, for better tracking and greater hull speed.

Mild rocker (river-running kayak)

No rocker (recreational or touring kayak)

Chine and Flare. Chine and flare describe the shape of a hull viewed head-on. Chine refers to the sharpness of the angle where the bottom becomes the sides of the boat. The hardest possible chine is a right angle. (Picture a flat-bottomed john boat.) The rounder the bottom, the softer the chine. Most downriver kayaks have soft chines, whereas freestyle boats have hard chines.

Flare refers to the curvature of the sides. A straight-sided boat has no flare, a design that produces very abrupt turns and tends to cause novice paddlers to capsize. Most whitewater boats have flared sides that gradually curve outward from the waterline to the deck.

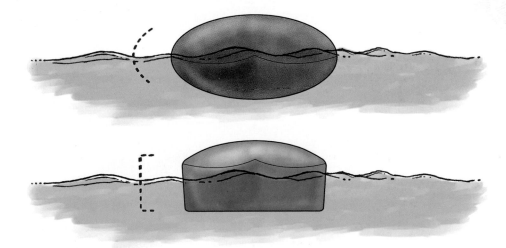

Top: *Boat with moderate flare and soft chine*
Bottom: *Boat with no flare and hard chine*

Stability. A boat's width, flare, rocker, chine, and length all affect its stability. Generally speaking, the more hull in contact with the water—especially in terms of width—the more stable the boat. Thus, a long, wide boat with no flare and a hard chine has the greatest initial stability, whereas a short boat with pronounced rocker, soft chine, and flared sides feels quite tippy. However, the most stable boat is not necessarily the easier one to paddle. Boats with flat bottoms and hard chines have good initial stability—they don't rock back and forth easily when sitting on flatwater. But lean them over too far, and they can flip suddenly. By contrast, a short kayak with soft chine and flared sides feels tippy when you're sitting in it, but it's actually easier to control in turbulent water. When you want to roll it over, you can—imagine trying to roll a ball rather than a box. With a little practice, though, you can bring either type of hull right-side up with a snap of the hips.

Like most decisions in selecting a boat, choosing hull design is a tradeoff. No single boat is ideal for everything. If you want a downriver boat to cover more miles with less effort, choose a longer hull with rounded sides. If you want to play your way down the river on waves and holes, a shorter, flatter hull will keep you entertained.

Materials. The vast majority of contemporary kayaks are made of rotationally molded ("rotomold") polyethylene, whose great advantages include strength, durability, lack of maintenance, and reasonable cost (and, to the boat builder, moldability). Because it stands up so well to abuse, rotomolded polyethylene is just about the ideal material for whitewater kayaks. Its only real disadvantage is weight. Fiberglass boats are about ten percent lighter than rotomolds, but are somewhat more expensive and fragile and require some maintenance. Kevlar and composite-material kayaks, mostly racing and high-end touring boats, are the lightest of all and very strong, but they are also very expensive.

WHITEWATER KAYAKS

The 1970s and '80s saw a boom in the use of kayaks in whitewater, as an expanding core of paddlers began to discover the thrills of surfing holes and waves, shooting falls, and just playing around on the river. The style of kayaking that evolved was to traditional paddling what snowboarding was to downhill skiing. The point was not how fast you got down the river, but in what style. Instead of finding the fastest route through a rapid, this new breed of kayakers was looking for the best wave or hole to surf.

Downriver kayaks like the Dagger RPM are the longest whitewater boats. They have displacement hulls for greater straight-ahead speed and better tracking than the short planing hulls of playboats.

The Dagger Juice is an example of a river-running playboat. This type of boat is a good choice for the aggressive beginner who wants an all-around whitewater kayak.

Once paddlers found out how much sheer fun was to be had in whitewater, and the more adventurous among them began inventing new moves and activities, kayak manufacturers responded with a variety of designs for specific uses. Although there are now endless variations on the basic theme, whitewater kayaks can be classified into four main types, according to the type of water and activity they're built for.

Downriver Boats. This is the classic kayak shape—longer than a playboat, with smoother lines. As the name indicates, downriver boats were originally designed for traveling down the river, going through rapids rather than playing in them. They are longer than playboats (8 to 10 feet) , have displacement or semi-displacement hulls (a compromise between the planing and displacement shape) rather than planing hulls, and therefore track better and have more hull speed than playboats and freestyle boats.

River-Running Playboats. This broad category includes boats suitable for both deft maneuvering and downriver paddling. Playboats are of medium length (7 to 9 feet). They have tapered but not ultra-thin ends and planing hulls with moderate rocker and flare. This category is the best compromise between user-friendliness and performance, and so is a good choice for the beginner.

Freestyle or Rodeo Boats. In the early 1990s, companies such as Dagger, Perception, and Prijon began making boats specifically for rodeo competition. These were designed for the experienced paddler who does tricks: surfing waves and holes, dipping and diving, and doing cartwheels, spins, enders, and loops. Freestyle boats are short (6 to 8 feet) and tend to have radical volume distribution—flat ends and bulbous middles. Squirt boats are the most extreme in this category; they have very short hulls, with thin front and rear decks that slice easily into the water during stunts.

Creek Boats. Creek boats are specifically designed for running extreme stretches of whitewater, including waterfalls. Creek boats have high-volume hulls, with the volume evenly distributed front to rear. The thick, rounded bows and sterns keep the boat riding high in frothing, tumbling drops, rather than cutting into the water as a freestyle boat is designed to do. This hull shape also lets the boat pop to the surface quickly after a big drop. The shape and buoyancy of a creek boat makes it forgiving of mistakes and therefore a good novice boat.

Freestyle kayaks have short planing hulls with extreme rocker. This model, the Dagger Kingpin Icon 6.3, is a freestyle competition boat just over six feet long.

Creek boats like this Dagger Nomad have thick, high-volume hulls for buoyancy in extreme whitewater drops. Note how much thicker this boat is in the bow and stern than the other kayak types.

Parts of a Kayak

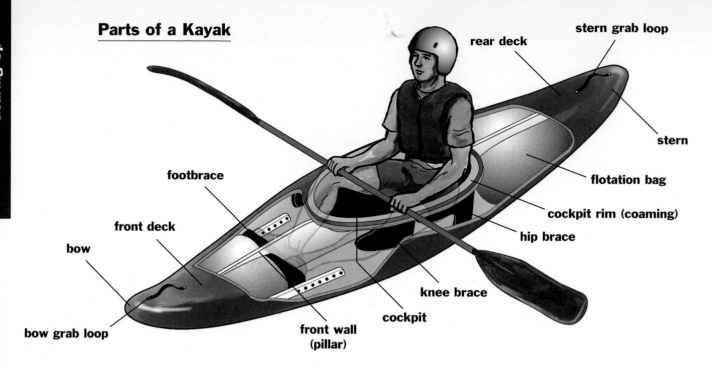

rear deck

stern grab loop

stern

flotation bag

cockpit rim (coaming)

hip brace

footbrace

front deck

bow

knee brace

cockpit

bow grab loop

front wall
(pillar)

ADJUSTING AND OUTFITTING YOUR KAYAK

A kayak should fit your body like a comfortable shoe: snug but not too tight. The boat should fit closely enough around your lower body that it responds to your hip and leg movements. When you lean into a turn, for example, you must be able to tilt the boat in that direction by dipping one knee and lifting the other; when doing an Eskimo roll, you must right the boat with a snap of your hips.

Some kayaks have seats that can be moved forward or back to accommodate people of different heights, and most have adjustable footbraces: blocks attached to the inside of the hull that can be moved forward or back by loosening and tightening screws. When adjusting your kayak, first set the seat position so that when you're settled in the cockpit, the boat is "trim"—it sits level in the water. Then, adjust the footbraces so that when the balls of your feet are resting on them, your knees are slightly bent and about a foot and a half apart, pointed outward toward the sides of the boat and resting snugly against the knee or thigh braces. Your heels should be almost touching and your toes should be pointed outward, toward the sides of the boat.

Many boats also have adjustable thigh, knee, and hip padding, but if not, you can customize your cockpit by gluing foam blocks in the appropriate places.

The goal of all this adjustment should be to achieve a snug fit without feeling jammed into your cockpit. You should have enough leg and foot movement to keep from cramping when you're relaxing on a flat stretch of water, and you should not be so wedged in that you can't do a wet exit (see page 20). If you can't

achieve this fit and wind up with a trim boat, you're in the wrong-size kayak. Try a different model.

An empty kayak filled with water will sink to the bottom of the river, a fact you'll discover the hard way if you're ever forced into a wet exit in whitewater and don't have flotation in your boat. Flotation bags are inflatable plastic bags that you stuff into the stern (and the bow, if there's room), in the spaces on either side of the wall (the "pillar") that runs down the center of the boat. You blow up the bags through a long inflation tube that then tucks out of the way. If your boat goes under, the inflated bags prevent water from filling the empty spaces; the boat stays afloat and can be easily pulled to shore.

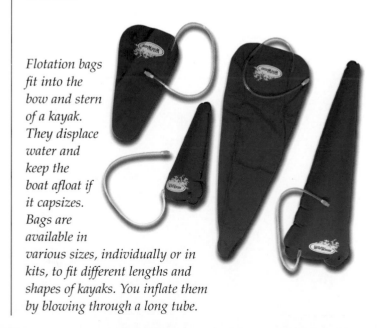

Flotation bags fit into the bow and stern of a kayak. They displace water and keep the boat afloat if it capsizes. Bags are available in various sizes, individually or in kits, to fit different lengths and shapes of kayaks. You inflate them by blowing through a long tube.

Unlike canoe paddles, kayak paddles are double-ended, and most modern ones are offset, or "feathered"—the blade at one end of the shaft is set at a different angle than the blade at the other end. This design makes for more efficient paddling, because as the one blade is pulling through the water with its broad side, the opposite blade is cutting through the air edge-first, reducing wind resistance. You'll appreciate this design most dramatically when you have to paddle any distance into a headwind. However, the offset design does require you to rotate your wrist as you switch sides, a technique explained in Chapter 3. Non-offset (unfeathered) paddles are available for those who find this wrist-turning technique difficult, and in recent years, whitewater paddlers have begun using paddles with less and less offset.

The most efficient blades are spoon-shaped, because a curved surface grabs more water than a flat one. The inside of the spoon is the side that, for most strokes, pushes the water—it faces the stern in a forward stroke—and is called the powerface. The other side, the outside of the spoon, is called the backface.

As is true of most outdoor equipment, the best paddles combine light weight with strength, whereas cheaper ones are either flimsier or heavier. Carbon composite and Kevlar paddles have the very best strength-to-weight ratio and are the most expensive. Nylon or fiberglass is less expensive and not quite as light and rigid.

Traditional kayak paddles have straight shafts, but bent-shaft models are now available that some paddlers find more comfortable and efficient. Also, multi-piece

shafts are available that twist together with ferrules, like a fishing rod. These shafts have the advantage of portability and interchangeability: you can switch blades or shafts to suit your needs. The disadvantage is that over time and hard use, the shafts tend to loosen at the ferrules. Multi-piece paddles are useful as spares because they're small enough to store in a whitewater boat.

Use the table below as a rough guide to paddle length, keeping in mind that other factors, such as your own arm length and strength, not your height alone, will influence which paddle length is best for you. Try out a paddle before buying it. Some store owners will let you test a new paddle and exchange it for one of different length, but if not, see if you can borrow a few paddles of different lengths to find which suits you best. In general, use a longer paddle for downriver paddling and a shorter one for playboating.

Good paddles are expensive—between $250 and $450—but lightweight and durable, so choose carefully and then buy the best one you can afford.

Your Height	Paddle Length
5' 0"–5' 4"	188 cm–194 cm
5' 5"–5' 7"	191 cm–197 cm
5' 8"–5' 10"	194 cm–200 cm
5' 10"–6' 0"	197 cm–203 cm
6' 1"–6' 3"	200 cm–206 cm

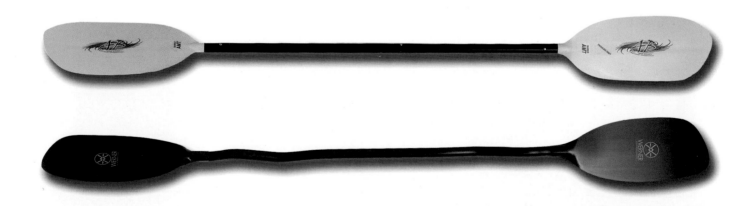

Top: *A four-piece straight-shaft paddle is useful as a spare because it can be stored inside the boat.*
Bottom: *A top-end carbon fiber paddle from Werner, with a bent shaft and foam core. The carbon fiber makes the paddle lightweight yet stiff, and the foam core makes it buoyant.*

OTHER ESSENTIAL ITEMS

Helmet

A good helmet is an absolute requirement for whitewater kayaking. It can prevent serious injury if you're thrown from the boat or if you roll and your head hits a rock, the boat, or any other hard object. Your head is especially vulnerable in fast water, which tends to be littered with rocks. A paddling helmet has an outer shell of plastic or composite material, a foam lining, and a chin strap. The most protective models cover the temples and ears, as well as the skull and forehead. Try on several models and sizes before buying. To test the fit, put the helmet on, fasten the chin strap, then push up on the front of the helmet. If it slides back, exposing your forehead, try a smaller size or a different model.

PFD

A Type III (vest-type) Personal Flotation Device is required by law for boaters in most states and by the American Canoe Association for participation in its courses. It's smart to wear a PFD any time you get into a kayak and it's an absolute necessity for whitewater paddling.

Get a PFD designed specifically for kayaking, rather than for general boating or water skiing. A kayaking PFD has armholes large enough to allow freedom of movement. The vest must be adjustable so that it won't slip up over your head.

Good PFDs start at about $40. Cheaper ones may meet basic safety requirements but will not fit as well and may chafe at the arms. Paddling all day in an ill-fitting or poorly designed PFD is torture.

Try on a PFD before you buy it. Sit down, adjust the side straps for a snug fit, and have someone pull up on the vest at the shoulders. If it slides above your head, try another model or one with a crotch strap. You should also simulate paddling movements by rotating your arms in wide circles, then crossing them over your chest. If the vest chafes or bunches up anywhere, try another size or model.

Spray Skirt

The spray skirt keeps water from seeping into your boat through the cockpit. It must fit both your body and the boat. The tunnel, the upper tube, should fit snugly around your waist, but not so tightly that it constricts your breathing; the skirt, the lower part, must snap securely around the rim of your cockpit. Some manufacturers make spray skirts for particular models of boats, but whichever model you choose, make sure it actually fits tightly around the cockpit of your boat before you buy it.

Neoprene is the best material for whitewater kayak spray skirts, because it's tougher and produces a more watertight seal than nylon, the material used for touring kayak spray skirts.

First-Aid Kit and Knife

Keep an outdoor first-aid kit in your boat. It can be stored in a waterproof container such as a drybag—a treated PVC sack with a watertight closure at the top. Drybags are available in several sizes from outdoor catalogs and paddling shops and can also be used to store wallets, cameras, binoculars, and so forth.

A locking-blade folding knife that clips to your vest can be a lifesaver if you ever get tangled in a rope during a rescue. A knife is also handy for custom-trimming the foam braces inside a boat.

A quality helmet is a requirement for whitewater kayaking.

For a whitewater kayak, choose a spray skirt made of neoprene. Since the purpose is to keep water out of your boat, the tunnel (the upper part) must fit your torso snugly, and the elastic cord at the bottom of the skirt must snap tightly around the rim of the cockpit. Note the large grab loop at the front of the skirt.

A PFD designed for kayakers, like this model from Lotus Designs, has extra-large armholes to allow for range of motion. Try on models at the shop to make sure you've got a good fit.

CLOTHING AND OTHER GEAR

Footgear

Neoprene booties or water shoes help keep your feet warm in cool weather, but you can get away with sport sandals or old sneakers if the water is warm enough. Whatever you choose, remember that you'll be carrying the boat from the car to the river, sometimes over rocks or gravel, and you may also be walking in a riverbed or scrambling up a rocky bank. Choose footgear with soles thick enough to protect your feet against rocks. However, be aware that there's not much room in the bow of whitewater boats—some are very small up front—so bulky footgear may be hard to get in and out of the boat.

Gloves or Pogies

Water can soften the hands and lead to blisters, and in cold weather, bare digits just don't function as well as gloved ones. For either reason, you may want to invest in paddling gloves. Pogies are mittens that strap to the shaft of the paddle. You put your hands through them to grip the paddle directly. This design prevents you from losing the gloves and also makes you feel more attached to the paddle.

Nose Clip

A nose clip is handy if you plan to do a lot of rolling, as it keeps water from being forced up your nose when you go under. Attach it to your helmet for easy access and to keep it secure.

Neoprene kayaking booties keep your feet warm and dry in the boat and also protect your feet when walking to and from the river and carrying the boat on portages.

A nose clip keeps water out of your nose when you roll the boat or capsize.

Paddling gloves keep hands warm and stop blisters from developing on water-softened skin. Pogies, mittens that strap to the shaft of the paddle, serve the same function as gloves—to keep your hands warm and dry. But because your hands go through them to grip the paddle shaft directly—your skin against the shaft— they give you a greater sense of control. They also make you feel more attached to the paddle.

Drysuits, Wetsuits, and Paddling Jackets

The drysuit is the warmest and most waterproof of paddling clothes, a loose-fitting garment of waterproof fabric with elastic gaskets at the wrists, ankles, and neck. Drysuits come as one-piece garments or as jacket/pants combos. When new and properly fitted, they seal out all water, and when worn over undergarments of fleece or polypropylene, they keep you warm. One-piece suits are, however, only necessary for the coldest weather, and do have the disadvantages of making you feel somewhat constricted and, in moderate weather, making you sweat. A two-piece drysuit gives you the option of wearing just the jacket in cool weather. One final caveat: drysuit gaskets wear out with time and must be replaced.

A wetsuit is the next-warmest option, a neoprene garment that allows a thin layer of water against your skin. This layer of water is quickly warmed by your body heat, making the wetsuit a comfortable choice in all but the coldest weather. Wetsuits come as one-piece overalls (Farmer Johns or Farmer Janes) or as separate shirts and pants.

Drysuits are made of waterproof fabric with gaskets at the neck, wrists and ankles. They are the most waterproof form of clothing, and, when worn over fleece undergarments, the warmest.

Wetsuits are snug-fitting neoprene garments that trap a thin layer of water between fabric and skin, a layer that is quickly warmed by body heat, keeping you comfortable in all but the coldest weather. The style shown is a Farmer Jane, the female counterpart to the popular Farmer John wetsuit overalls.

Finally, most paddlers invest in a paddling jacket, a waterproof nylon shell that can be worn by itself or over a wetsuit or other type of top. This combination gives you three-season protection against the elements.

Whatever you choose to wear, avoid cotton. It takes forever to dry and loses all its insulating value when wet. The most common weather-related affliction in paddling is hypothermia, the cooling of core body temperature to a dangerously low level, and the most common cause is prolonged exposure to cold water. The inexperienced boater is especially vulnerable in the spring and fall, when the air temperature seems warm enough to wear light clothing but the water is still cold. A typical scenario is that a boater soaks his cotton T-shirt during the day and is still wearing a wet shirt when the temperature drops in the evening.

For an extra layer in cool weather, wear a long-sleeved polypropylene T-shirt or a fleece pullover under a paddling jacket or drysuit top.

A paddling jacket of lightweight, waterproof fabric is an essential piece of clothing for cool or wet weather.

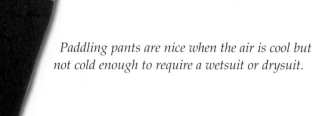

Paddling pants are nice when the air is cool but not cold enough to require a wetsuit or drysuit.

2
Fundamentals

This chapter contains the basics that will get you on the water with the least amount of trouble and start you off paddling with good form. The first thing you'll have to do is carry the boat down to the water and launch it. You'll also need to become learn how to attach and remove the spray skirt.

Beyond that, take time to study the positions and moves described in this chapter. These fundamentals of movement and posture are so basic and universal that understanding them may be the single most valuable lesson in your paddling education.

Lifting and Carrying a Kayak

To carry your boat, lift it onto your shoulder and crook your arm into the cockpit, with your hand holding on to whatever interior brace is available. Your arm just holds the boat in place; your shoulder carries the weight. If you have to walk some distance to the put-in, even a light boat may cut into your shoulder, so experiment with balance, moving the boat fore and aft to find the most comfortable position. You can also put a sponge or a piece of foam on your shoulder for cushioning.

Standard Lift

1. Grab the front inside rim of the cockpit to lift the boat off the ground.

2. Bend your knees and slip your arm into the cockpit.

3. Swing the boat onto your shoulder and stand up.

The Knee-Kick Pick-up

A neat trick for getting the boat onto your shoulder is to bump it up there with your knee.

1. Grab the side of the cockpit.

2. Lift the boat onto your knee.

3. Kick your knee up to raise the boat onto your shoulder.

4. Ready to roll.

Attaching the Spray Skirt

Before you go anywhere in a whitewater kayak, you must attach the spray skirt to make a watertight seal. Otherwise, your boat will fill with water when waves wash over the deck or when you do an Eskimo roll.

Put the spray skirt on your body at the car, when you're donning the rest of your gear. (Yeah, it feels a little funny walking down to the water in something that looks like a tutu, but you'll get used to it.) Before attaching the skirt, make sure the gasket is rotated so the grab loop is in front, where you can reach it in a wet exit. This is crucial. If the boat flips and you can't roll it upright, you must be able to extract yourself from the cockpit quickly, and the first step in removing your spray skirt is yanking on the grab loop.

3. When the back is attached, stretch the skirt forward to seal it around the cockpit rim. (You can use one of two techniques to complete the seal. You can stretch the gasket forward, snap it on the front, and then finish by pressing it in place on the sides. Or, you can work forward, pressing along the sides with your elbows and finishing by snapping it on the front.)

1. Step into the tunnel and pull up the skirt. It's a good idea to grab a bunch of material when pulling up the skirt, so you don't stretch the neoprene. When you're boarding the boat, pull the tunnel up to chest level and fold the back of the skirt inward so you don't sit on it.

2. Reach behind you and press the gasket into place on the back of the rim.

4. Once the skirt is in place, double-check that the grab loop is in front and that you haven't tucked it under the seal.

Shore Launch

A shore launch is done by simply getting into the boat on land and pushing yourself into the water. Roto-molded polyethylene hulls are virtually indestructible, so you can do a shore launch over most surfaces—even tree roots—without damaging the boat. (Avoid banks with sharp rocks, however.)

1. Set the boat down on the bank, get into the cockpit, and attach the spray skirt.

2. Push yourself into the water.

3. Launched!

Water Launch

If the bank is not suited to a shore launch—if it's steep or rocky—or you don't want to put surface scratches on your pristine hull, use a water launch.

1. Place the paddle across the deck, right behind the cockpit, with the far blade over the water and the near blade resting on shore. If you're facing the boat with the bow pointing to your left, reach down with your right hand and grasp the paddle shaft, wrapping your fingers over the shaft and around the lip of the cockpit rim.

2. With your left hand, grab the other end of the shaft on the near side of the boat. Thus braced, sit down on the back deck of the kayak.

3. Then put one leg at a time into the cockpit, straighten your legs, and push yourself forward into the seated position, with your feet on the pegs.

Posture and Torso Rotation

Although we will soon show techniques for individual strokes in detail, you will benefit greatly from understanding a few general principles of body mechanics and posture that apply to all strokes. If you apply them well, right from the beginning, you will be a more effective, powerful, and injury-free kayaker.

The three cardinal rules of kayak posture and body movement are:

1. Sit up straight, without leaning forward or backward. A straight-up posture is especially important in river running, because leaning back increases the water pressure on the stern of the boat and increases the likelihood of a flip. Remember, though, that sitting up straight does not mean sitting rigid. Don't tense your muscles.

2. Keep your head over the center of the boat.

3. Perform strokes by rotating your torso rather than by reaching with your arms.

These principles are interconnected: a straight-up, balanced posture lets the body rotate more freely.

Why torso rotation? Power. Your abdominal and back muscles are much stronger than your arms, and if you learn proper technique—if you execute strokes by rotating your torso rather than by reaching with your arms—you'll go faster and farther with less strain. This is the same principle that a boxer uses to deliver a powerful punch or a slugger uses to hit a homerun: each athlete generates power by rotating his waist and hips.

To illustrate the concept for yourself, stand in front of a wall with your shoulders square to it. Position yourself so that with your arm extended straight out in front of you, your fist is six inches from the wall. There are two ways you can reach the wall. You can lean forward at the waist till your fist touches it, or you can remain upright and touch it by rotating your torso. Assuming you wanted to hit the wall hard, which technique do you think would deliver the most powerful punch?

When you're out on the water, remember the rules of posture and torso rotation, and think of your back and abdominal muscles as the engine that drives the boat and your arms simply as the link between the engine and paddle blade.

Correct posture, with torso erect and head centered.

Incorrect posture. Don't lean back.

Leaning the Boat

Leaning or "edging" the boat is an essential skill in kayaking. You do it by shifting your lower body, not by leaning your upper body out over the deck. Your upper body should remain vertical, which will keep your center of gravity directly over the centerline of the boat. Your mantra should be: lean the boat, not your body.

To lean the boat, keep your hips loose and lift one knee while pushing down with your opposite buttock. As the boat leans, your body should stay perpendicular to the waterline, not to the deck of the boat, so you must be flexible at the waist. (This is sometimes called the "J-Lean," after the shape made by your torso and the boat.) The farther over the boat leans, the more flexible you must be at the waist to keep your torso perpendicular to the water.

For effective leaning, keep your knees spread and slightly bent. Place the balls of your feet on the footbraces with your heels together and toes pointed outward. You use your lower body to lean and balance the boat, and this wide stance maximizes side-to-side control.

To lean the boat to your left side, press down with your left buttock while lifting your right knee (and vice versa).

Leaning your body over the side of the boat . . .

Keep your torso upright and your head over the center of the boat.

. . . will cause you to capsize.

Tuck Position and Wet Exit

Before you do any whitewater paddling in a kayak, you've got to know what to do when the boat flips. Note the wording: not "if" the boat flips, but "when." Whitewater kayaks tend to turn upside down, sometimes because you intend them to, other times not. Though this is a potentially dangerous position, it's one you can easily get yourself out of. In fact, righting a capsized boat or just rolling for the sheer fun of it will soon become routine. However, there will be situations where you can't roll an overturned boat, either because you haven't yet mastered the technique or for some other reason beyond your control. In these situations, you must know how to extract yourself from the cockpit.

First, sitting in your boat on shore or in calm water, practice what is known as the tuck position. Simply lean forward at the waist as far as you can, as if trying to touch the deck with your nose. On the river, you should get into this position the instant you roll over. For one thing, it protects your head from rocks and other underwater hazards as you're swept along.

The tuck position

After you've flipped, the next step is to perform a wet exit, which is the process of pushing yourself out of the cockpit. You can practice the first part—the spray skirt release and the basic movements of your hands and legs—on land.

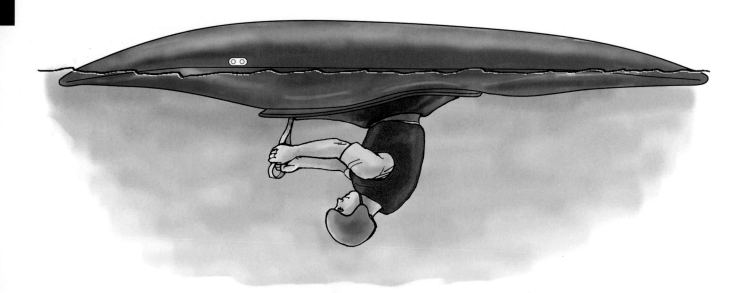

1. First, you must free the spray skirt from the kayak. You may need to lean back to access the skirt; nonetheless, try to remain as close to the boat as you can. Release the spray skirt by grasping the grab loop. Pull it up and away from the cockpit rim and then back toward you to release the sides and back.

2. Still leaning forward, place your palms on the deck on either side of the cockpit, outside the spray skirt. Relax your legs and feet so they no longer press against the inside of the boat, and, keeping your legs straight, push yourself out of the boat.

The final part of the maneuver—which is like doing a straight-legged somersault out of the boat—is a lot easier underwater, and you should practice it there before you go paddling. With a friend by your side, paddle into waist-high water that has a smooth, hazard-free bottom (no rocks or snags). Take a deep breath, lean your upper body to the side until the boat flips, and complete the first two steps of the exit.

3. Then, push the boat away from you with your legs. Once you're free of the boat, your PFD will pop you to the surface. The most common beginner mistake in a wet exit is trying to get out of the boat by leaning back in the cockpit and swimming to the surface. This strategy just tangles your legs. Somersault out of the cockpit and push the boat away from you with your legs before heading for the surface.

You may be wondering what to do with the paddle during all this. You can hold onto it after you flip, grasping it in the middle with one hand while releasing the grab loop with the other. Then, still holding the paddle with one hand, you can place it lengthwise against the hull as you push off the sides of the cockpit with both hands. Alternatively, you can let go of the paddle when you flip and try to recover it at the surface.

Mastering the wet exit before you go out on the river is not only a necessary safety precaution. Knowing you can extract yourself from the boat also gives you the confidence to paddle in water that might otherwise be intimidating.

The Hip Snap

The hip snap is simply a quicker, more forceful version of the basic movement used to lean a boat. It is the most powerful force you can apply to bring a boat level again, and is thus an essential skill for whitewater kayaking—the key component in braces, rolls, and Eskimo rescues.

Once you get the hang of leaning the boat, as described on page 19, you can practice the hip snap by rocking the boat from side to side, edging it over as far as you can without capsizing, then snapping it back into place with hip action: lifting your on-side knee (i.e., the knee on the side toward which the boat is leaning) while lowering your off-side buttock. Remember to keep your torso vertical and let your lower body do the tilting.

Practice the hip snap first by leaning the boat from side to side . . .

. . . and snapping it upright with your hips . . .

. . . keeping your upper body perpendicular to the water's surface.

The next step is to practice righting an overturned boat with the hip snap in a controlled situation, where you can hold onto the edge of a pool or the deck of a friend's boat. The key difference between righting a leaned boat and a capsized boat is that in the latter case, you must keep your head *down* until your hips have righted the boat. This is counterintuitive, because when a boat overturns and your head is underwater, your instinct is to raise your head immediately to grab a breath. The problem is that this motion counteracts the momentum of the hip snap and makes it much harder for you to right the boat. Instead, keep your head down until the boat and your torso are upright. Your head should be the last thing to come up.

Practicing the Hip Snap

1. While hanging onto the bow of a partner's boat (or the edge of a pool), lean the boat over until your body is in the water.

2. Keeping your head down, use your hips to snap the boat upright.

3. Keep your head down throughout the righting phase. Don't bring it up until your boat is completely level.

The Eskimo Rescue

The Eskimo rescue is a technique for righting a capsized boat using a hip snap and the bow of a nearby boat as support. If you've not yet mastered rolling (see page 52), this is the handiest way to right your boat, and it's a lot quicker and more convenient than doing a wet exit and swimming to shore. However, it does require that another boat be nearby and that the paddler in that boat knows you need his or her assistance.

1. With a partner's boat nearby, get into tuck position.

2. Roll the boat over.

3. Thump on the bottom of your upside-down boat. This signals the rescue boat to paddle to your boat and put its bow up against your hull.

4. When you feel the rescue boat touch your boat, sweep your hands along your hull until you find its bow. Grab it . . .

. . . and use a hip snap to right your boat.

Remember to keep your head down until your boat is completely level.

Vision

Vision—looking where you want to go—is a less concrete yet still fundamental paddling skill, one often overlooked by beginners intent on the details of technique. Take a global view. Rather than focusing on your hands or on the bow of your boat, keep your head up, and look ahead to where you're going in the river. This approach lets you see hazards before they're right on top of you and also lets you scout the best routes while you still have time to make decisions.

Concentrating on the big picture also has a physical advantage in stroke technique. If you look where you're going—that is, if you turn your head in the direction the stroke is taking you—your eyes will lead your head, which in turn will lead your torso, maximizing your body rotation and power.

Attitude

One more thing: be positive. Visualize success. Confidence cannot be manufactured out of thin air, of course, and one must bring fundamental skills and an appropriate level of caution to the river. But like all sports, whitewater kayaking can be a huge boost to the spirit, especially if you go into it with a positive attitude. If you believe you can do something, you probably can.

3
Stroke Basics

Paddle Grip and Technique

PADDLE DESIGN

Most whitewater kayak paddles, as described in Chapter 1, have curved, offset blades. A curved blade produces a more powerful stroke than a flat one because it grabs more water. This design means, however, that a blade has a right and wrong orientation. For most strokes, the concave side, or powerface, should push against the water and face the stern. Also, when using an offset paddle, you must rotate the shaft as you switch sides so the powerface of the blade enters the water at the correct angle on each side of the boat.

If you are using a paddle with straight blades, mark one side of each blade as the powerface, so you can consistently apply the stroke instructions that follow.

27

HAND SPACING

To find the right hand spacing on the paddle shaft, hold the paddle in front of you with your forearms bent at a 90-degree angle (or slightly less) to your upper arms and adjust your grip so that each hand is the same distance from the nearest paddle tip. Both the elbow angle and the positioning of hands are important.

Grip the paddle so each hand is the same distance from the nearest blade.

The 90-degree elbow angle results in the right amount of paddle extending beyond your hands on either side. If your hands are too close together, too much shaft will extend beyond them, costing you power and control. Conversely, if your arms are spread too wide, you won't have the reach you need to control the boat.

Maintaining the equidistant spacing is also important, because if one hand is closer to the blade tip than the other, the strokes on that side will have less leverage than those on the other, and the boat will veer. Once you've established this spacing, you may want to mark your hand positions with a piece of tape around the shaft where your thumbs are resting. Even experienced paddlers' hands tend to migrate while paddling, and a visual reference is helpful.

SLIP HAND AND CONTROL HAND

One end of an offset paddle is designated the control end, and the other the non-control end. (Most paddles are right-hand control.) The control hand is fixed on the shaft, whereas the non-control (or slip) hand lets the shaft rotate within it.

Here is how the system works with a right-hand control paddle: Visualize a paddler switching sides while doing forward strokes. His right hand holds the shaft so that when his wrist is straight, the blade goes into the water on the right side of the boat with the powerface facing rear. When he lifts the paddle out of the water to switch sides, he cocks his right wrist back, maintaining a firm grip on the shaft there, while loosening the grip with his left hand to let the shaft rotate until the blade on that side is at the proper angle. He then tightens his left hand while executing the stroke on that side. Thus, the general rule is that the control hand maintains its grip on the shaft while the non-control hand lets the shaft rotate within it.

Avoid the common error of letting the shaft rotate in both hands as you switch sides. The control hand's grip should remain fixed as a reference point; otherwise, the blade angle will become skewed when you switch and the powerface won't face squarely to the rear when

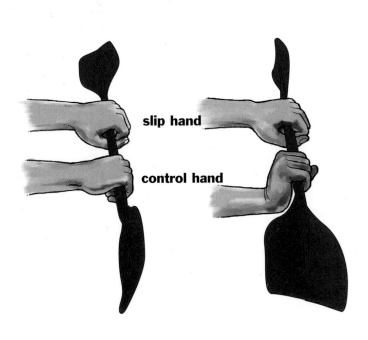

slip hand

control hand

**Wrist cocked out /
cocked back**

Wrist cocked in

Left: *When you are stroking on the control-hand side of the boat, neither wrist is cocked.*

Right: *If you are using an offset paddle, when you lift the blade from the water to switch to the other side, cock the wrist of your control hand (the right, for this paddler) out while loosening the grip of your slip hand to let the shaft rotate. This allows the blade to enter the water at the proper angle. Just before putting the blade in the water on the opposite side, tighten up the grip of your slip hand to keep the blade at that angle for the stroke.*

Stroke Basics

you put it in the water. If you maintain your control hand grip, the powerface on that side will always be correctly oriented and you can adjust the blade angle on the non-control side by cocking your control wrist.

One other tip: don't hold the paddle *too* tightly. A death grip on the shaft will soon cramp your forearms.

BLADE ENTRY, ANGLE, AND DEPTH

For maximum efficiency, the blade should face squarely in the direction you're pulling, not angled one way or the other, and it should be immersed to the point where it meets the shaft. You want as much surface area as possible pushing directly against the water. Also, don't begin pulling on the blade until it's completely immersed.

The easiest way to tell if you've got an efficient blade entry is to listen. A quiet stroke is an efficient one—the paddle blade should not make a splash when it enters the water. A clean entry produces a more powerful, efficient stroke. Stab or slice the blade (depending on the type of stroke, a little of each may occur) into the water as if you were using a knife. Either using a bad angle or pulling on the blade before it's completely immersed will produce a noisy stroke.

VERTICAL VS. HORIZONTAL SHAFT

The more horizontal the paddle shaft is during a stroke, the more the boat will turn. The shorter the boat, the more dramatically it responds to turning strokes, and whitewater kayaks—being the shortest craft on the river—are particularly sensitive in this regard. Thus, if want the boat to go straight (as in a forward stroke) you must keep the shaft as vertical as possible, whereas if you want a boat to turn (as in a sweep stroke) you must keep the shaft more horizontal. Put another way, the blade should travel closely alongside the hull throughout a power stroke, whereas it should reach out in a wide arc for a turning stroke.

In practice, there are infinite angles at which you can hold the paddle in a stroke, which you will learn to adjust depending on what you want the boat to do.

ON-SIDE AND OFF-SIDE

The side of the boat on which a stroke is being executed is called the on-side, and the opposite side is called the off-side. These terms are often used in stroke instructions to specify positioning of body parts or the direction of a turn. For example, if you are doing a draw stroke on the right side of the boat, that side is the on-side, and the instructions will tell you to "lift your on-side knee" to keep the boat level during the stroke. Likewise, a forward sweep is described as one that "turns the boat sharply to the off-side," i.e., toward the side opposite of that on which the stroke is being done.

Use a vertical paddle for power strokes . . .

. . . and a horizontal paddle for turning strokes.

The forward stroke, or power stroke, is the most basic in your repertoire, and most expert paddlers have good ones. Do not skim over the fundamentals for this stroke. Learning good form at the outset will pay dividends all your days on the water. As you proceed with this stroke, keep in mind the principles of posture and torso rotation from the previous chapter: sit upright and gain power by rotating your torso rather than by reaching with your arms.

    For instructional purposes, this stroke is separated into four phases: wind-up, catch, propulsion, and exit. In practice, these steps are inseparable: do not pause between them, but let them flow together as one movement.

Stroke Basics

Wind-up. Rotate your torso and extend your on-side arm (in this picture, the left) forward, keeping it almost straight, while holding the off-side arm higher and bent at the elbow. Avoid bending forward at the waist. The torso rotation at this crucial phase of the forward stroke is like winding a big, powerful winch. When you unwind it, the power you generate will pull the boat toward the paddle.

Catch. Sitting upright with your on-side arm straight, plant the blade in the water as far forward as your torso rotation will comfortably allow. Keep the shaft as vertical as possible. Plant the blade right next to the hull, knifing the edge into the water so there is no splash. Remember: a quiet stroke is an efficient stroke.

Propulsion. Once the blade is fully immersed, unwind your torso as you pull with your bottom arm and punch forward with the opposite one (in this case, the right.) Keeping the shaft vertical and your on-side arm straight, bring the blade back toward your hips, moving it right alongside the hull all the way. Don't let the blade wander away from the boat, or you'll be doing a sweep stroke, which will turn the boat and decrease the efficiency of your power stroke. Also, keep the blade squarely facing rear, not angled one way or the other.

Think of this phase as the act of pushing your feet rapidly past the paddle blade, rather than as pulling the paddle rearward. Let your torso rotation—not your arm—pull the boat toward the paddle. Arm weariness after an hour on the river usually indicates a tendency to move the boat by pulling with bent arms, which is bad form.

Note how the shaft is vertical and the blade is close to the hull during the propulsion phase of the forward stroke.

Exit. Stop the stroke at your hips . . .

. . . and remove the blade cleanly by slicing it up out of the water. Continuing a power stroke back beyond your hips is counterproductive: it doesn't push the boat forward but turns it.

You are now in position to begin the next stroke—after you complete a forward stroke on one side, you then do one on the other side, then back again, and so on. Remember that in switching sides with an offset paddle, your control hand (the hand on the side you began with) maintains its grip on the shaft while the slip hand (the one on the opposite side) rotates. The control hand must be cocked back to turn the opposite blade at the correct angle before it hits the water on the other side of the boat.

KEEPING THE BOAT STRAIGHT

You will almost certainly experience side-to-side veering when you put together your first forward strokes. A whitewater kayak's responsiveness to strokes is a two-edged sword: the same design features that make the boat maneuverable also make it hard to keep moving in a straight line. Keep in mind the following points as you work to maintain forward motion.

EQUAL LEVERAGE ON BOTH SIDES

Check your hand spacing on the paddle shaft to make sure each hand is the same distance from the blade, that one side is not getting more leverage than the other. A common beginner's error is traveling hands; use tape to mark equidistant positions if necessary. Try to apply the same amount of force on each side of the boat. Most people are stronger in one arm than the other, and so naturally pull a little harder with their dominant arm. This effect is diminished by relying on torso rotation, rather than arm pulling.

POSTURE AND BALANCE

Avoid leaning and rocking the boat from side to side as you switch paddling sides. Leaning the boat increases the effects of a slight turn; if a boat has a certain momentum in one direction (i.e., it has begun to veer), leaning the hull presents more surface area for the water to push against, and the boat continues turning more readily than it would if it were flat. Rocking side to side or front to back also produces a slower, less efficient ride because this motion wastes energy that might be used in going forward.

CORRECTING EARLY

The further the boat gets into a veer, the harder it is to correct, so try to sense when you're going off course and correct early. A quick sweep or stern draw (see Chapter 4) or even consecutive forward strokes on the same side will often do the trick.

REVERSE STROKE   Moves the boat backward

The reverse or back stroke is very useful, not so much to travel somewhere in reverse as to reposition your boat before a move or to back away from trouble. The basic stroke is essentially a mirror image of a forward stroke, except that you can't reach as far back as you can forward.

Leaning back when doing this stroke buries the stern in the water and slows the boat's rearward progress. Maintain a generally upright posture; if anything, lean slightly forward.

Note that the backface (the non-power face) of the blade becomes the powerface for this stroke. In other words, you're pushing water with the convex, not the concave face. Although this blade orientation makes for a less powerful stroke, the goal of a reverse stroke is usually not power but quick positioning, so don't bother rotating the shaft. Reverse strokes are usually followed by turning or forward strokes, and your paddle will be correctly oriented for these strokes if you haven't rotated it.

Wind-up. Rotate your torso back without leaning backward at the waist. Notice that the shaft is horizontal at this point, although it will soon become vertical.

Catch. Move the shaft to a vertical position and plant the blade just behind your hips. As in the forward stroke, slice the blade into the water without a splash.

Propulsion. Unwind your torso and push the blade forward toward your knees, keeping the shaft vertical and moving right alongside the hull.

Exit. Slice the blade out of the water when it's about even with your knees. Pushing the blade farther forward will cause the boat to turn.

4
Turning Strokes

Whitewater kayaks turn very easily, so you won't need much effort to get results from the strokes described in this chapter. However, paying attention to the basics of form will give you more powerful strokes and let you put the boat where you want it more quickly and efficiently. Keep in mind the basic principle of paddle angle from Chapter 3: the more horizontal the shaft—the smaller the angle between shaft and water—the more turning power the stroke will have. This is the exact opposite of the rule for power strokes, where you keep the shaft vertical to increase forward thrust and reduce veering.

35

SWEEP STROKES

Sweep strokes take their name from the sweeping motion of the paddle as it travels in a wide arc from bow to stern, or vice versa. Sweep strokes are the best way to turn the boat when you want to preserve your forward (or backward) momentum. They are easy to learn, as they require no arm or torso contortions, and they bring dramatic results in a kayak.

FORWARD SWEEP	Turns the boat sharply to the off-side while maintaining its forward momentum

We show two versions of this stroke, one for short boats with planing hulls (playboats, rodeo boats), and the other for longer boats with displacement hulls (downriver boats). The first version travels a shorter distance, because planing-hull boats turn so easily, whereas the second version is a longer stroke, because long displacement hulls are more resistant to turning.

Planing Hull

Wind-up. Rotate your torso forward with your on-side arm straight, extending the paddle blade as far forward as you can without bending forward at the waist or reaching with your arms. The shaft should be nearly horizontal. Note how the paddler is looking in the direction of the turn.

Catch. Plant the blade cleanly as close to the bow as possible, immersing the paddle to the throat before pulling.

Propulsion. Push away from the bow while rotating your torso and swing the paddle in a wide arc toward the stern.

Exit. When the blade is alongside your hips, slice it out of the water. Note how far the bow has swung to the right from the starting point at the wind-up.

Displacement Hull

Wind-up. Same as for a planing hull: rotate your torso and extend the paddle as far forward as is comfortable.

Catch. Plant the blade near the bow, as close to the boat as possible.

Propulsion. Once the blade is immersed, unwind your torso . . .

. . . bringing the paddle in a wide arc toward the stern.

Exit. Bring the paddle all the way to the stern before slicing it out of the water. Note how the stroke finishes significantly farther back than in the previous sequence.

Wind-up. Rotate your torso back for the catch.

Catch. Slice the blade fully into the water at the stern.

Propulsion. Rotate your torso forward and sweep the blade out and away from the stern.

Continue toward the bow in a wide arc, keeping your sweep arm straight.

Exit. Lift the blade out of the water at the bow . . .

. . . and prepare for the next stroke.

Turning Strokes

DRAW STROKES

A draw stroke pulls the boat toward the paddle and, depending on the path of the draw, can be used to pull the boat directly sideways or to turn it left or right. Experienced paddlers use many varieties of the draw, altering the paddle angle during the pull to position the boat exactly where they want it.

An inherent challenge in using draw strokes is balance: the catch position requires extending both arms out over one side of the boat, the top hand almost directly over the lower. To counteract this shift in weight, you must keep your torso upright and lift your on-side knee. Keeping the boat as level as possible will not only prevent capsizing but increase the efficiency of the stroke.

SIDE DRAW   Pulls the boat directly sideways, toward the paddle

The side draw is useful for side-slipping around an obstacle while keeping the bow of the boat pointed in the same direction, or simply for repositioning the boat.

Wind-up and Catch. Rotate your torso toward the on-side and plant the blade as far out from the boat as you can by extending your on-side arm straight out and reaching across your body with your off-side arm bent at the elbow. Get the paddle as close to vertical as possible. Lifting your on-side knee will help keep the boat level. The more you rotate your torso, the easier it will be to reach across your body with your top arm.

Propulsion. By the time you start the power phase of this stroke, the paddle should be nearly vertical, with your top hand almost directly over your lower hand. Punching out with your top hand and pulling with your lower, draw the blade directly toward your hip— or rather, pull the boat toward the paddle. Imagine you're trying to drive your hip through the paddle blade.

Exit. Stop the stroke when the blade is about 6 inches from the side. (Pulling it all the way to the boat may cause you to capsize.) Cock the wrist of your control hand in (see the illustration on page 28) to rotate the blade 90 degrees, so its edge, not its face, is facing out from the hull.

Feathering Recovery. Slice the blade out through the water to begin another draw stroke. To demonstrate the correct blade angle, the paddler here has lifted the blade out of the water, but you can bring the paddle all the way back to the catch position underwater if the blade is properly angled.

As you extend the paddle out to do another draw stroke, rotate the blade back to its catch position.

Close-up of Feathering Recovery

These three photos show the wrist cocking in to rotate the blade for the exit/recovery phase of a side draw stroke.

Two versions are shown, the closed-face and open-face. Adjusting the blade angle between these extremes will help you hit the right balance between turning the boat (open-face) and maintaining momentum (closed-face), depending on the circumstances. Typically, the closed-face draw is used with planing-hull boats, which turn more easily but don't keep their momentum. The turning power of the open-face draw is often needed for turn-resistant displacement hulls.

Closed-Face

Wind-up and Catch. The body motion is the same as for the side draw: rotate your torso toward the on-side and plant the blade as far out from the boat as you can by extending your on-side arm straight out and reaching across your body with your off-side arm. Unlike the side draw, the blade should be angled so the leading edge is pointed toward the bow.

Propulsion. Pull the paddle toward the bow of the boat, rather than straight back toward your hip, as in the side draw.

In effect, you are pulling the bow of the boat toward the paddle while maintaining your forward momentum.

Exit. Slice the blade out of the water when it nears the bow of the boat.

Open-Face

Wind-up and Catch. Put the paddle in the water with the blade angled between 45 and 90 degrees away from the bow of the boat. You will need to cock back the wrist of your control hand so the powerface of the active blade will be facing the bow of your boat.

Propulsion. Unwind your torso and push the bow toward the paddle blade.

Remember to keep the boat relatively flat to maximize its rotation.

Exit. Lift the blade out of the water just before hitting the bow of the boat, or continue into a forward stroke. Notice how much farther the boat has turned than in the closed-face sequence.

This is a particularly useful stroke for steering or initiating turns in longer displacement-hull boats and also for reducing the momentum of a spin to your on-side.

Wind-up and Catch. Rotate your torso toward the on-side, as in the side and bow draws, and plant the blade as far from the boat as you can reach.

Propulsion. Rotate your torso rearward, pulling the blade toward the stern. Following the path of the blade with your eyes will help you rotate more freely. Remember: the eyes lead the head, which in turn leads the torso.

Exit. Just before the blade hits the stern of the boat, lift it straight up out of the water.

Turning Strokes

Like a side draw, the sculling draw pulls the boat sideways, but in this case you move the paddle back and forth with the blade submerged. You must experiment with blade angle when trying this stroke. If you angle the blade too much, the boat will spin rather than be pulled sideways. To start, use your hip as the center point of the stroke. If your boat spins toward your on-side, move the center point back. If your boat spins to your off-side, move the center point forward. Keep the boat as level as possible during this stroke.

To demonstrate paddle angles, the blade in these photos is held partly out of the water, but when doing the actual stroke, keep the blade fully submerged throughout the entire sequence.

Wind-up and Catch. As in the side draw, rotate your torso toward your on-side, your lower arm extended and your upper arm bent at the elbow and held high, reaching across your body. Plant the blade a little closer to the boat than you would in a side draw.

Forward Slice. Cock your wrist out until the powerface is angled 45 degrees away from the boat, and slice the blade forward until it almost comes out of the water.

Turning Strokes

44

Reverse Direction. When the blade is just past your knees, cock your wrist in to reverse the angle of the powerface.

Rearward Slice. Slice the blade rearward until it's again almost out of the water, and you've completed one cycle of the sculling draw.

From here, you can just continue sculling, bringing the blade back to the bow and then to the stern, going back and forth with the blade until you pull the boat where you want it to be.

The rudder is not a stroke, per se, but simply a way to steer the boat by dragging the paddle in the water at the stern and levering the blade one way or the other. Depending on the angle at which you hold the blade and how you move it—in a sweep or a draw motion—you can steer the boat left or right. For illustration purposes, the active blade is once again slightly out of the water; in practice, it would be completely submerged.

This is the basic paddle position for a rudder. Hold the blade vertically in the water and close to the boat, keeping it as parallel to the boat as possible. This keeps the boat tracking straight forward.

Cocking your wrist out angles the leading edge of the blade away so the boat moves toward the off-side.

Cocking your wrist in angles the leading edge of the blade toward the boat so the boat turns toward the on-side.

Turning Strokes

5

Braces and Rolls

Braces and rolls are moves used to keep a boat from capsizing or to right it after it has already flipped. Keep these basic purposes in mind when learning the moves, so you don't overuse them. Some beginners brace at the first threat of a capsize, but when you brace, you stop stroking. A moving boat can be steered, while a still boat is at the mercy of the river, so it is generally better to keep stroking and only resort to a brace as a quick defensive maneuver when a tip is inevitable.

Similarly, many beginners only think of rolling in terms of fun—as a cool move to be learned for the thrill of it. In fact, paddling instructors say that rolling is the first skill many beginners want to learn. Nonetheless, you'll have a lot more fun on the river if you first learn the basic mechanics of balance, posture, and torso rotation that allow you to keep the boat upright and take you where you want to go.

Even with the best of technique, though, you'll find yourself in situations where you must brace to keep the boat upright or roll to bring it right-side up again. Both braces and rolls require a strong hip snap to provide the final righting power, so you should review that technique (page 22) before learning these moves.

BRACES

The low and high braces are techniques for keeping a capsizing boat upright by pushing the flat of the blade against the water to counteract the momentum of the flip. Keep in mind two basic principles of paddle movement in bracing. First, a moving blade offers more support than a stationary one, because it uses more surface area; move the paddle blade toward you or in a sweeping motion when you brace. Second, the farther you place the paddle blade from the boat, the more leverage you will gain (but remember to keep your weight centered over the boat as much as possible.)

LOW BRACE   Prevents a capsize to the on-side

The basic low brace position: elbows bent and held above the shaft, resembling a push-up. The backface of the paddle faces down.

To practice the low brace, lean the boat to your on-side and place the backface of the paddle against the water, as far from the boat as you can reach. Your weight should be centered over the boat.

As you draw the paddle toward the boat, begin a hip snap by lifting your on-side knee and dipping your off-side buttock. Lowering your head helps set the boat flat on the surface.

Complete the hip snap. Don't raise your head until the boat is level again. The body and paddle still need to be over the center of the boat.

The low brace in practice, maintaining balance on a wave. Note the position of the elbows above the shaft.

HIGH BRACE   Prevents a capsize to the on-side

The high brace performs the same function as the low brace—it stops a capsize—but involves a few key differences in technique, the main ones being that the elbows are held below the paddle shaft and the powerface hits the water. Since this is the position in which the paddle is held for most strokes, the transition from a stroke to a high brace is smoother and quicker than to a low brace, and the high brace is therefore the more common maneuver. You can go from a stroke to a high brace back to a stroke very smoothly, and the high brace can also be applied in a greater variety of situations, but it does not provide quite the initial stabilizing power of a low brace, because the paddle face is not as flat to the water.

Never bring your elbows above the shaft or your hands above your head when high bracing, as these positions make your shoulders vulnerable to injury, including dislocation. If your arms are held high and away from your body when the paddle blade is in turbulent water, the force of the water can shove your shoulder sockets out of joint. Shoulder dislocation is a common whitewater injury, but it can be avoided by keeping your upper arm close to your body when the paddle is in the water.

The basic high brace position: elbows held below the paddle shaft, with the powerface of the blade facing down.

As boat leans, keep the paddle shaft above your elbows. Your top hand should stay below eye level.

Extend the on-side blade, powerface down, onto the surface of the water.

Press the on-side blade down on the water and begin a hip snap toward the off-side, keeping your head down and sliding the paddle shaft across the cockpit.

Complete the hip snap to right the boat, staying balanced over the center.

The high brace in practice, transitioning to a forward stroke.

ROLLS

Once you've learned the hip snap and the braces, you have the basic tools you need to roll a kayak. Although a roll can be done just for the fun of it, its practical applications are more important. For one thing, rolling is a lot quicker and easier than doing a wet exit, then swimming the boat to shore and emptying it. For another, once you learn to roll a kayak, you'll be more confident in whitewater, free to explore new locations and try moves you'd otherwise avoid.

General Tips for Rolling

- Practice first with a partner in calm, warm water at least waist-deep. A swimming pool is ideal.
- Wear a nose-clip to avoid getting a noseful of water. You may also wear a face mask, so you can watch what's happening underwater.
- First master rolling in one direction—toward your dominant arm, or in whichever direction feels more comfortable. Try rolling in the other direction only after you've mastered the basic techniques.
- Make smooth, deliberate movements underwater, rather than fast, jerky ones. Many first attempts at rolling fail because the paddler panics once he's upside down and rushes to get his head above water. To gain confidence, try holding your breath on land. Exhale, take a deep breath, and then watch the second hand of your watch. See how easy it is to hold your breath for 30 seconds? That's two or three times the breath you'll need to roll a kayak. So relax. Once the kayak is upside down, take a second to visualize what you're going to do, and then do it slowly and smoothly.

- Keep your head down until the boat is level again. The most common error in rolling technique is raising the head too soon.
- Keep your paddle blade near the surface as you sweep. Sweeping the paddle too far under the surface ("paddle diving") prevents the torso from coming up.
- Before starting your sweep out, punch your hands to the surface beside your boat until you feel air on both hands.

Preventing Paddle Diving

Here are three tips to prevent your paddle from diving when rolling:

1. As you sweep out, push your sweep arm upward.
2. Keep the sweeping blade flat, parallel with the surface, to reduce water resistance.
3. Keep your inside arm (the arm opposite the sweeping arm) bent at the elbow and close to the boat. Raising and/or straightening this arm will cause the opposite blade to dive.

Entire books have been written on rolling, and there are a dozen techniques and variations. (Collectively, they are referred to as "the Eskimo roll.") We show two basic rolls here. As a general rule, the C-to-C roll works well for flexible paddlers and displacement hull boats. The sweep roll works well for paddlers with limited flexibility and planing hull boats. It's recommended that you try them both and use the one that works best for you.

C-TO-C ROLL   Rights the boat after a flip

The C-to-C rights the boat primarily through a sudden and powerful hip snap, aided by a sweeping high brace. This roll is so-named because the change in the curve of the spine provides the righting force. You begin with your spine in a C-shaped curve toward the water, and as you right the boat it shifts to a curve in the opposite direction. In essence, this is a continuation of the hip snap and Eskimo rescue techniques—you're just using your paddle to right yourself rather than another boat.

The C-to-C roll is powered by the shift that occurs in a hip snap.

Executing the C-to-C Roll

After tipping the boat upside-down, place your paddle parallel to the hull, above the surface of the water, with the powerface of the front blade facing down. At this point, your torso should be bent forward in tuck position. The farther you can extend your off-side arm across the hull of the boat, the easier it is to reach the surface with your on-side paddle blade.

Begin sweeping the blade out, keeping it at or near the surface. Note that the off-side arm is bent at the elbow and close to the hull.

As the sweeping paddle comes perpendicular to the boat, begin a strong hip snap by first leaning your torso toward the surface and relaxing your off-side knee (here, the left). Note the off-side arm is still bent and tight against the hull and the shaft is angled to prevent the sweeping blade from diving. Also note that the paddler's head is still in the water; you must resist the impulse at this stage to raise your head and gasp for air.

Continue the strong hip snap, pressing down with your off-side buttock and lifting the on-side knee to roll the boat upright under you. Your head should still be down.

Almost there, but the head is still following the body.

The righted boat at the end of the roll.

The sweep roll is very similar to the C-to-C but involves sweeping the paddle in a longer arc toward the stern and rotating the torso to follow the sweep. The sweep roll is a bit easier to learn, as it requires a less powerful hip snap and is generally a more fluid sequence.

Place your paddle parallel to the overturned boat, the same as for the C-to-C roll.

Begin sweeping away from the boat with the on-side blade, keeping it close to the surface.

Begin your hip snap while continuing to sweep the paddle toward the stern. Be careful not to pull the paddle down. The quicker the blade travels to the stern of the boat, the more effective the roll.

Continue the hip snap while following the sweeping blade rearward with your head and torso. (This is the main difference between the sweep roll and the C-to-C roll.)

Raise your head only when the roll is complete.

6

On the River

READING THE RIVER

As a whitewater kayaker, you will be navigating fast water in a small boat, so you must learn to read the river. You will need to be able to recognize surface features—waves, eddy lines, holes, upstream and downstream Vs—and what they signal about the features beneath. This knowledge, in turn, requires a basic understanding of how water behaves in a riverbed: What happens when fast water hits a submerged obstacle? What causes a wave to form in a river? How do changes in the volume of water affect the river?

One way to gain this knowledge is by spending a lot of time on the water and making a lot of mistakes. A better way to begin is by studying some basic principles of the physics of moving water.

FORCE OF THE CURRENT

Three factors affect the force of the current: the gradient of the riverbed, the width of the riverbed, and the volume of flowing water.

Gradient

Gradient is the slope of the riverbed, expressed in the number of feet it drops per mile. A steeper riverbed creates a faster current. A very rough rule of thumb is that gradients of less than 30 feet per mile produce mild whitewater, up to Class II (see International Scale of River Difficulty, pages 78–79), and that gradients between 30 and 60 feet per mile produce Class III and IV rapids. However, since gradient is an average over the

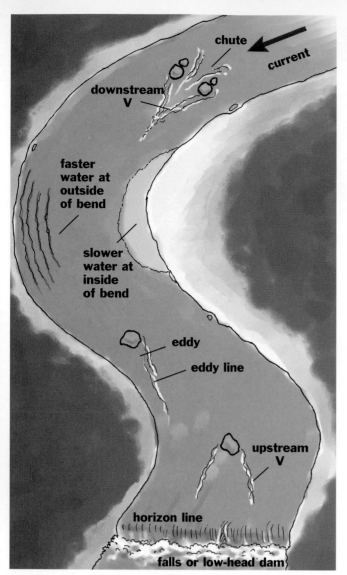

Common river features

length of a mile, you can't tell the character of a particular stretch by this number alone. A river with a moderate gradient may be flat for a long way and then plummet fifty feet. On the other hand, a river with a relatively high gradient may have a constant rate of drop over its entire length and produce fast water but no major hazards.

Another significant point about gradient is that the force of the water increases at a greater rate than gradient: if the gradient doubles, the force quadruples. Thus, even a slightly steeper stretch of river will be many times more powerful than a flatter stretch.

Flow

Flow is the volume of water carried past a point in a fixed amount of time, expressed in cubic feet per second (CFS). Unlike gradient, flow is variable: it changes in response to rainfall and dam releases. A river's CFS is crucial because, like gradient change, a change in volume

has a profound effect on the force of the water: if the flow doubles, the force triples. Thus, a creek that's an easy float in June may have dangerous rapids in May. And at any time, torrential rain or a dam release can transform a placid river into a drowning machine.

Many of the most popular whitewater rivers in the United States are dam-controlled, including the Ocoee and Nantahala in North Carolina, the New and the Gauley in West Virginia, the Upper Youghiogheny in Maryland and Pennsylvania, the Kern and American in California, and the Colorado through the Grand Canyon. Local boaters become well-acquainted with dam-release timetables, and anyone who runs such rivers should seek this information.

Another point to consider about flow is that a significant increase in volume changes the character of river features important to paddlers. At high volume, rocks that are normally exposed become buried under the surface, and where once there were eddies, now there are holes. Eddy lines (see page 62), the key feature in the paddler's waterscape, vanish. So before running a river, check river levels in local newspapers, paddling club websites, or boat shops.

Gradient and flow are related and must be considered together when evaluating the risk of a river. A river with a relatively low gradient—one that drops 20 feet per mile, say—may still be very powerful if it has a high-volume flow. Conversely, there are relatively low-volume streams with very steep gradients—several hundred feet per mile—that make them impossible to run.

Width

Current speed is also affected by the width of the river. As the river narrows, the current speeds up, because the same volume of water is being squeezed through a tighter channel. A narrows or canyon may also have turbulent water where the currents from the wider stretch slam together.

CURRENT LANES

The current is faster in the middle of a straight stretch of river because there is less friction there than against the banks. The water in the middle also tends to be deeper, with fewer obstructions. However, when a river goes around a bend, most of the water is thrown to the outside, creating much faster current there and slower current on the inside. The fast current erodes the outsides of bends, undercutting banks and dredging deep channels, whereas the slow current on the inside of the bend drops sediment and debris there, forming bars and shallower water.

Because of this current differential in river bends, the most fun is to be had on the outside, but that's also where the hazards are—the downed trees and undercut banks. So keep your head up when approaching a bend. If you want to get to the inside, you've got to take action early; unless you do something, your boat will be swept to the outside.

ROCKS AND OTHER HAZARDS

Rocks, the most common obstacle in whitewater, are responsible for creating the holes, waves, and eddies that experienced kayakers seek. The size, shape, and depth of rocks in the current determine how water behaves as it flows around and over them, and the froth, waves, or current lines around a rock will tell you how to approach it. You should learn to recognize a few basic patterns.

A large, rounded rock with its top above the surface has a buildup of water called a pillow on its upstream side where the oncoming water hits. The pillow is a benefit to the paddler because it pushes a boat away from the rock. On the downstream side there may be a pocket of lower water and an eddy—an upstream flow circulating water back into the pocket.

A large rounded rock with its top above the surface has a "pillow" of water on its upstream side where the water hits it.

A rock with an undercut face has no pillow: the water flows around the rock beneath the surface. Any obstacle with an undercut face is extremely dangerous in fast water because it can suck a boat against it and trap it there. If you see a large rock in a swift current with no pillow above it, steer clear.

A rock with an undercut face has no pillow because the water flow is drawn beneath the surface around the rock.

If you're being swept into a rock or other obstacle, lean into it. Although your instinct may be to lean away, doing so lowers the upstream deck of the boat to the onrushing current, a position that may cause the boat to flip or to be pinned against the rock with such force that you won't be able to free yourself. But if you lean downstream, into the rock, the current will be pushing against the rounded bottom of the boat and won't have as much pinning force. Also, by leaning this way you'll be able to fend off the rock with your paddle or arms and continue downstream.

If you are swept into a rock, lean into it. The pillow on the rock's upstream face will help push your boat away, and you can also reach out and fend off the rock.

Downstream and Upstream Vs

The water pointing downstream in a smooth, V-shaped tongue is the path to follow: it points to a channel between rocks, also known as a chute. Conversely, upstream Vs point to obstacles. Learn to recognize this pattern as you look downstream from your vantage point in the boat and plot a course following the downstream Vs.

Holes and Hydraulics

A hole is the paddler's term for the depression just downstream of a submerged rock into which water is recirculating. A rock below the surface of a fast river is marked by a pillow of water just upstream of it and some degree of turbulence right behind it, from froth to waves. Holes can be entertaining rides or hazardous traps, depending on the size and position of the rock and the volume of water pouring over it. It's very easy to get into them—the current just sucks you in—but it can be difficult or impossible to get out. In checking out a hole, you must evaluate its size, shape, and the amount of water involved.

current

A large volume of fast water flowing over a large submerged rock or ledge can create a hole: a depression with a strong recirculating current. Depending on their size and shape, holes can be places to play or dangerous traps.

Smaller holes are marked by short lengths of backwash behind them and perhaps a standing wave just downstream. These holes are relatively safe to run. More challenging and potentially dangerous holes form when a significant volume of water pours over a large rock or ledge, creating a recirculating current called a hydraulic. The most severe hydraulics are called "keepers" because they literally keep boats in them. One way to gauge the power of a hydraulic is to note the length of the eddy behind the rock or ledge. If the water behind a large submerged rock is moving back upstream from more than three feet away, you're headed into a powerful hole.

Another element to consider in assessing a hole is its shape, because this determines how you'll get out. If the sides of the hole are farther downstream than the middle, then the hole is said to be "smiling." It will be easy to exit because you can paddle out either side into the main current. If, however, the hole's sides are far-

ther upstream than the middle, it is said to be "frowning." A frowning hole is dangerous because you must fight an upstream current to paddle out of it.

Particularly deadly hydraulics form below low-head dams. These dams may not appear dangerous; they're just low concrete walls with a smooth flow of water going over. But the volume of water is actually huge, and the force of the hydraulic this creates, as well as the fact that it stretches all the way across the river, creates an inescapable trough. Stay away from low-head dams or any holes so wide that they offer no routes of escape.

The Dock Street Dam on the Susquehanna River in Harrisburg, Pennsylvania, has claimed eleven lives since 1985. Most fatal low-head dam accidents occur when upstream boaters approach too close and are swept over, thrown out of the boat, and drowned by the powerful hydraulic.

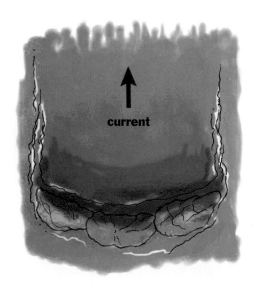

current

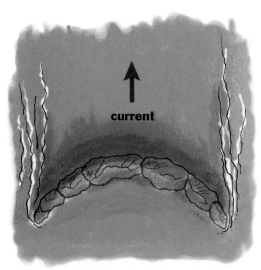

current

Left: *A smiling hole is relatively easy to escape by paddling to either side of the main flow.*

Right: *A frowning hole is more dangerous because the boater must fight the current to get out.*

Horizon Lines

A level, unbroken line of water across the river downstream of you may mean danger. It can signal a precipitous drop—a ledge, falls, or low-head dam—over which a large volume of water is flowing. Either the drop or the hydraulic behind a horizon line is a potential killer, and if you get too close, the strong current just above the ledge can pull you over. Learn to recognize horizon lines visually from upstream, and listen for the sound of a large volume of water going over a ledge. Paddle to shore and portage around or scout a safe route.

If you see an unbroken line across the water, as in this boat-level view taken upstream of Wesser Falls on the Nantahala River, pull over and scout the water ahead. A horizon line can signal a dangerous drop-off or low-head dam.

This is the view from the bank 100 feet downstream of the previous photo, showing Wesser Falls, Class IV water that only expert paddlers in whitewater boats should attempt.

Strainers

A strainer is an underwater object, commonly a downed tree, that allows water to flow through it. Strainers are extremely dangerous because they "strain" the water while trapping objects—including people and boats—too large to pass through them.

Downed trees are the most common form of strainer—any obstacle through which water flows but which can trap a boat or a person. Downed trees are commonly found in the swift water on the outside of river bends.

Along wooded rivers, strainers are most often found on the outside of bends, where the fast water undercuts banks and uproots trees. Other submerged objects, including fences, cables, grates, or debris deposited by floods, can act as strainers and may be found anywhere in the river. Ask local paddlers about such hazards.

Rising water is another factor that can create strainers by covering brush and trees along the bank. Keep an eye on the river ahead, and stay away from strainers.

Waves

Unlike waves on lakes or seas, which travel across the water, waves in a river are stationary. They're created when fast-moving water hits the slower-moving water below it. This happens in a few different situations. A standing wave forms where a sheet of water plunging over a submerged rock or through a chute between rocks hits the slower water just below.

If the wave is tall enough to break back on itself, it's called a stopper, because it can literally stop a boat. Holes often have stoppers below them, but such holes aren't as dangerous as hydraulics because enough water is flowing through the hole to push your boat downstream after it's momentarily stopped by the wave.

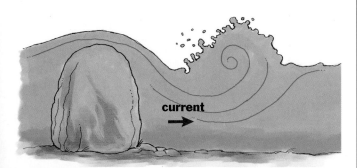

Stopper waves are those that are steep enough to crash back on themselves. So-named because they can literally stop a boat, stoppers are favorites of advanced whitewater kayakers, who seek them out for surfing and other play moves.

A wave train is a regularly spaced series of waves that occurs where deep, swift water is squeezed into a channel and piles up on the slower-moving water downstream. Wave trains are relatively safe to run because there are no rocks beneath them. In fact, they mark the channel and, hence, the best route to follow. The key to recognizing a wave train is the even spacing of the waves. A wave off by itself or out of alignment with the series marks a rock.

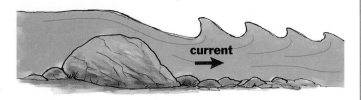

A wave train is a regularly-spaced series of waves that occur where deep, swift water is squeezed into a channel and hits slower-moving water. Wave trains normally mark the channel and are a safe route to follow downstream.

EDDIES

An eddy is a teardrop-shaped area of water behind a rock or other obstacle. The significant feature for boaters is that an eddy has an upstream flow, a phenomenon created when water rushing downstream around a rock sucks the water from directly behind the rock, creating a depression that the downstream water rushes back to fill. An eddy line marks the boundary between these upstream and downstream currents.

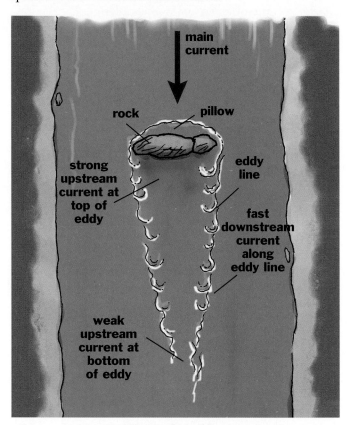

Parts of an eddy

Recognizing eddies and getting in and out of them are the most basic skills in paddling rivers. In most cases, eddies are safe havens. Boaters use them as resting places and as stations from which to scout the river below. As we have seen, the lengths of eddy lines can also signal the power of the hydraulics that created them—another important reason to learn to recognize them.

An eddy forms behind an obstacle, with the tip pointing downstream. An eddy's upstream current is strongest at the top, right behind the obstacle. The farther from the obstacle, the weaker the upstream current becomes, until eventually it dissipates altogether and joins the downstream flow. Of particular significance to boaters is the fact that the downstream current is strongest right next to the eddy line. Some instructors call this the "rejector line," because if you don't cross it with enough speed or at the right angle, it will push your boat back into the main current.

On the River

When paddling in whitewater, keep four general rules in mind:

1. Paddle aggressively. To maintain control in moving water you must move the boat faster than the current. Once you lose your forward momentum, you go where the current takes you. It is not enough to float along and steer; you must point the boat where you want it to go and propel it there.

2. Lean the boat into turns. A combination of forward momentum and a weight shift in the direction of the turn will steer a boat much more effectively than even the strongest turning strokes in a slow-moving boat riding flat on the water.

3. Maintain a downstream lean when crossing the river. When you're traveling diagonally or directly across the river, lift your upstream knee to lean the boat slightly downstream. A boat tilted this way presents its rounded bottom, rather than its edge, to the oncoming current, letting the water flow under the hull. If you lean the boat upstream, the current can catch the edge of the boat and flip it.

You may note a seeming contradiction to this rule in the instructions for eddy turns on page 64, where you are told to lean the boat upstream as you enter the eddy. However, these instructions are consistent with Rule Number 3—because an eddy current flows in the opposite direction of the main current, you're actually leaning the boat in the direction of this current, or "downstream" within the eddy itself.

4. Look ahead to where you want to go. Fix a visual goal in your mind. If you're doing an eddy turn, look across the eddy line into the eddy itself and where you want the boat to arrive. If you're ferrying across the river, look to your destination eddy on the far shore rather than focusing on the rock right in front of you or the square foot of water where you're planting your paddle. This kind of vision will help you plan the best route and use the current to your advantage.

PLANING AND DISPLACEMENT HULLS ON THE RIVER

As you have seen, planing-hull boats react differently to river currents and paddle strokes than do displacement-hull boats. Planing hulls are a bit slower and tend to turn very easily, whereas displacement hulls are faster and track better. This difference in performance means a slight but significant difference in technique when doing river moves. An essential part of the eddy turns, peel-outs, and other moves on the following pages is crossing eddy lines at the proper angle. The strong current differential at an eddy line can cause the slower planing-hull boat to spin out, so you need to approach the line at a greater angle (between 60 and 90 degrees) and use forceful forward strokes on the inside of the turn to punch across it. A displacement-hull boat, on the other hand, moves across the eddy line more quickly and is not as easily turned by the eddy line. Because of the greater speed, you can approach the line at less of an angle (about 45 degrees) and use a sweep or forward stroke on the outside of the turn to get across. Notice that in the photo sequences on pages 65 and 66, the two boats approach the eddy line at different angles but end up in the same place.

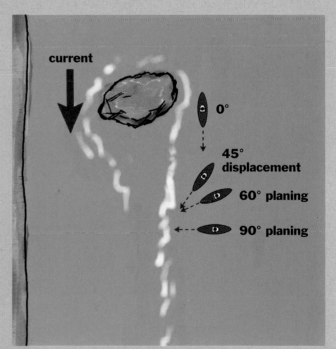

For the moves on the following pages, vary your entry angle according to the type of hull you have.

Cutting out of the main current into an eddy—the eddy turn—is the most fundamental skill in river running. It requires a basic understanding of eddy anatomy (see the illustration on page 62), along with the ability to paddle decisively and to lean your boat effectively. The formula for eddy turns (as well as peel-outs and ferries) is: Angle, Speed, and Lean. If you've positioned your boat correctly as you approach the eddy, and if you hit the eddy line at the right place with some momentum and the correct lean, the turn works like gravity—rather than frantically fighting against the current, you harness the river's force. The boat just falls into the eddy.

Angle

Aim to hit the eddy line just downstream of the rock, at an angle between 45 and 90 degrees, depending on the

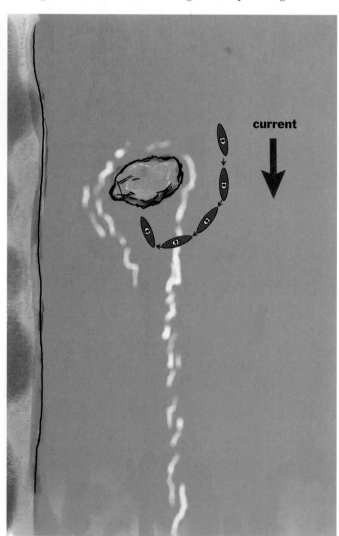

Enter the eddy at its upstream end, just beyond the rock or obstacle that creates it, and punch across the eddy line with at least a 45-degree angle.

type of boat you're in. Setting this angle involves the vision principle mentioned previously: before the river carries you past the rock, you must have positioned the boat far enough out from the eddy line that you can turn into it at the right angle, yet not so far away that you'll be swept past the eddy entirely. You want to hit the eddy where its upstream current is strongest, right behind the rock. If the angle is too great—more than 90 degrees—the main current may sweep your stern downstream. If your angle is too little—if you're nearly parallel to the eddy line—you won't be able to punch through it.

Speed

Paddle hard across the eddy line. You've chosen your entry point behind the rock because the upstream current is strongest there and will pull your bow into the eddy. But the downstream current is also strongest right outside the eddy line, just before you cross it, so you'll need some hull speed to punch across.

Lean

Remember the mantra: lean into turns. For eddy turns, this means leaning upstream. At the moment your bow hits the eddy line—just when you feel the eddy current start turning your bow upstream—lift your downstream knee and sink the opposite buttock to carve the boat into the eddy. The mechanics of turning are key here. If you lean your body instead of the boat, or lean the wrong way—away from the turn, downstream— you may flip the boat.

Strokes for Eddy Turns

Strokes are most important in the set-up phase of eddy turns, when you're still in the middle of the river trying to fix the point and the angle at which you'll hit the eddy line. Once you hit that line, hull speed and boat lean will take care of the turn itself. But as you approach the eddy line, you may have to adjust the boat's angle with a quick, powerful stroke. For example, if you find your approach angle is too little you'll need to do a sweep stroke on the downstream side of the boat to turn the bow upstream and achieve a better angle for punching across the eddy line. Conversely, if your angle is too great—if you're more than perpendicular to the eddy line as you approach it—you'll need to decrease that angle with a sweep or forward stroke on the upstream side of the boat.

Eddy Turn (Planing Hull)

Plan your approach so you'll hit the eddy high (near the downstream edge of the rock) at an angle between 60 and 90 degrees to the eddy line, and power toward it with strong forward strokes.

Take a forward stroke on the upstream side of the turn as you punch across the eddy line. Look upstream at the rock—as always, your head leads your torso.

Lean into the turn, carving the boat across the eddy line. Note the head and torso pointed at the rock. Maintain pressure on the forward stroke to keep the boat moving forward.

Cross the eddy line, still leaning into the turn. Hold the lean until the boat stops sliding sideways in the eddy. At this stage, both planing and displacement hull boats are at about the same spot in the eddy.

Paddle toward the rock, into the heart of the eddy.

Eddy Turn (Displacement Hull)

Plan your approach so you'll hit the eddy high (near the downstream edge of the rock) at an angle of about 45 degrees to the eddy line, and power toward it with strong forward strokes.

Take a sweep stroke on the downstream side of the turn as you punch across the eddy line. Looking upstream at the rock will help put your torso in the right position to guide the boat upstream. (Compare the entry angle here to the planing-hull version on the previous page.)

Lean into the turn, carving the boat across the eddy line. Note how the paddler's head and torso are pointed at the rock and his forward stroke is on the upstream side of the boat.

Cross the eddy line, still leaning into the turn. Hold that lean until the boat stops sliding sideways in the eddy.

Paddle toward the rock, into the heart of the eddy.

A peel-out is the maneuver for leaving an eddy and getting back into the main current. It is simpler than the eddy turn because you don't have to set up an angle while you're moving. But peel-outs do require more powerful initial strokes than eddy turns, because you're starting from a standstill and don't have the main current pushing you as you do when approaching an eddy. However, the same angle-speed-lean formula applies.

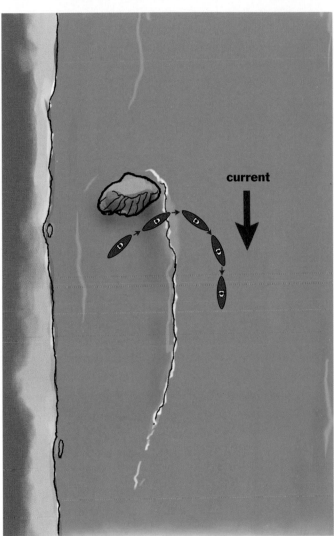

Start well within the eddy, and with the boat angled upstream, head towards the spot at the head of the eddy where you first entered. Lean into the turn and let the current swing the boat downstream.

Angle

Exit the eddy at about the same place and angle—45 degrees or more—that you entered it. Your starting point is key. Position the boat as far back in the eddy as you can without getting out of its upstream current. Being far back gives you distance to build up momentum for breaking across the line, and gives you enough room to prepare a proper angle for exiting.

Speed

Breaking across an eddy line, whether leaving or entering the eddy, takes forward momentum, but in a peel-out you don't have the current pushing you. Starting from a standstill within the eddy, you need powerful forward strokes to gain speed. So solid form—strong torso rotation, using your body and not your arms to generate power—is essential.

Lean

Just before you hit the eddy line, lift your upstream knee and shift your weight to your downstream side to lean the boat into the turn. If your boat is flat when it hits the eddy line, the main current can catch its edge and flip you. In fact, the failure to lean downstream soon enough is the most common cause of capsizing in peel-outs. Once you break across the eddy line, the main current will catch the bow, turning it downstream. Keep leaning downstream until the boat straightens out and is up to speed in the main current.

Strokes for Peel-Outs

Just like eddy turns, peel-outs require strong forward strokes to break through the eddy line. Just before you reach the main current, you'll need to switch strokes. Your choices will depend on the kind of boat you're using. A displacement-hull kayak often calls for strokes or sweeps on the upstream side to help with turning. A planing hull, on the other hand, will be turned more easily by the current, and you should maintain a forward stroke on the downstream side in order to keep the boat moving past the eddy line.

Peel-Out (Planing Hull)

Set up far back in the eddy.

Build up speed with strong forward strokes, and begin to lean the boat downstream as you approach the eddy line.

Continue leaning the boat downstream as you punch across the eddy line at an angle between 60 and 90 degrees. Plant a forward stroke on the downstream side to drive the boat across the eddy line and into the main current.

As you cross the eddy line, look downstream and continue to lean in the direction of the turn as you keep pressure on the downstream forward stroke.

Continue carving the boat downstream using either a forward stroke or a stern draw at the hip.

Once you're in the main current, headed downstream, you can level the boat.

Peel-Out (Displacement Hull)

Set up well within the eddy.

Build up speed with strong forward strokes. Begin to lean the boat downstream as you approach the eddy line.

Lean the boat downstream as you punch across the eddy line at about 45 degrees. Plant a sweep or forward stroke on the upstream side to drive the boat across the eddy line and into the main current. Using this upstream stroke will help initiate the spin of the boat downstream while continuing the forward momentum out past the eddy line.

As you cross the eddy line, look downstream and continue the lean in the direction of the turn as you take a forward stroke (or bow draw) on the downstream side of the boat. This downstream stroke will keep the boat moving forward and give some stability at the same time.

Continue carving the boat downstream using a forward stroke.

Once you're in the main current, headed downstream, you can level the boat.

A ferry is a maneuver for crossing a river from one eddy to another without moving downstream. It's an important skill, for you'll often find yourself in situations where you need to go directly across the river to set up for a run through a rapid or to get a better approach to a play spot. The ferry begins with a move similar to a peel-out and ends with an eddy turn, but in between requires you to set the correct angle to arrive at your target.

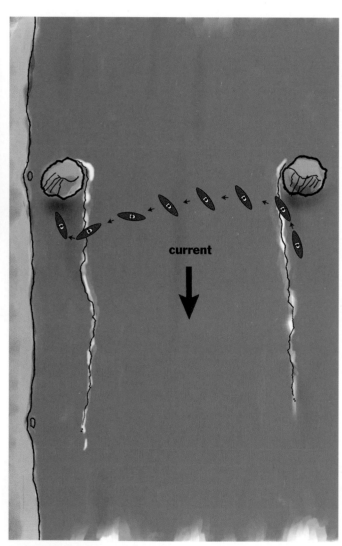

current

Exit the eddy much like you would for a peel-out, but keep the boat angled upstream as you move across the river. Use a properly angled eddy turn to enter the destination eddy.

Angle

Setting and maintaining the right angle as you cross the river is crucial in ferries. You must be pointed upstream, because if you try to paddle directly across the river, the current will take you far downstream of your target. The swifter the current, the more upstream your angle must be. It is always better to set an angle too far upstream than too far down, because it's easy to let the current swing your bow downstream but very hard to push it back upstream.

Once again, your starting point is crucial. Position the boat as far back in the eddy as you can without getting out of its upstream current, and stay no more than a foot or so inside the eddy line. This rule is especially true for beginners. Err on the side of too little angle. If the current is really ripping, point the boat almost directly upstream at the beginning of the ferry, and let the bow swing down as you cross. For most ferries, the right exit angle is about 20 degrees for displacement hulls, up to 45 degrees for planing hulls. However, the particular angle varies with current speed, river width, and the paddler's strength.

Although a ferry begins with a move like a peel-out—paddling out the side of an eddy into the main current—here you don't want your bow to swing downstream as it crosses the eddy line, but to head across the river at an upstream angle. Therefore, you'll need to plant a strong forward stroke on your downstream side just as you cross the eddy line to counteract the force of the main current.

Once you're headed upstream in the main current, you start paddling with forward strokes, letting the bow swing to between 45 and 60 degrees upstream.

Speed

Since you're beginning with what is essentially a peel-out, be sure to build up enough speed to break past the eddy line.

Lean

Lean the boat downstream during the ferry so the current doesn't catch the edge of your boat and flip it. When you get to the eddy on the far side of the river, shift your weight to your upstream knee, as in an eddy turn, as you cross the eddy line.

Standard Ferry

Set up in the departure eddy.

Punch across the eddy line, setting an upstream angle. (This ferry is being done in a displacement-hull boat. A planing-hull boat would exit with slightly more angle to avoid spinning back into the eddy as it crosses the eddy line.)

Let the bow swing downstream as you cross, but still maintain an upstream angle in the main current. Remember that without enough angle, you may be swept downstream of your target by the time you cross the river. Planing-hull boats need to be pointed a bit more upstream at this stage because they have less hull speed and therefore do not get across the river as quickly as displacement boats.

As you approach the destination eddy, let your bow swing downstream to set the right angle for an eddy turn. If you hit the eddy line pointed too far up-stream, the eddy-line current will reject you and push you back into the middle of the river.

Punch across the destination eddy line, reversing your lean to upstream, as in an eddy turn.

Home free.

Back Ferry

The back ferry is a maneuver for moving across a river or avoiding an obstacle. Unlike the standard ferry, where you angle the boat upstream and use forward strokes, the back ferry uses reverse strokes with the boat facing downstream.

In the photo sequence, the boater uses a back ferry to avoid a rock and then continues back-ferrying across the river to an eddy.

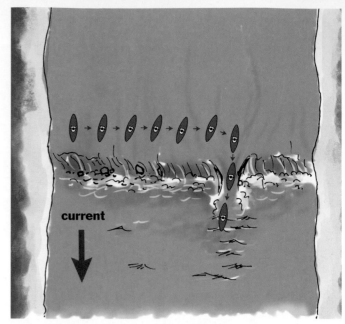

Use reverse strokes and careful leaning to move your boat laterally across the river toward an eddy, chute, or other target.

The paddler turns the stern of the boat away from the rock with a reverse sweep.

To move clear of the rock, he does a reverse stroke on the other side of the boat, maintaining a downstream lean.

Clear of the rock, the paddler keeps the boat moving diagonally across the current with the stern pointed upstream.

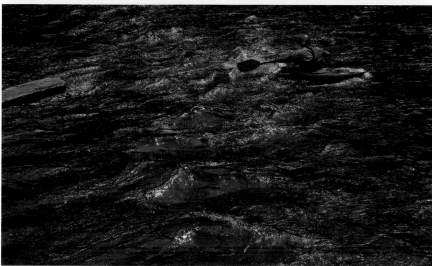

To avoid a flip, he maintains a slight downstream lean as he crosses the river—he leans slightly forward (an exception to the vertical-posture rule) and lifts the upstream knee.

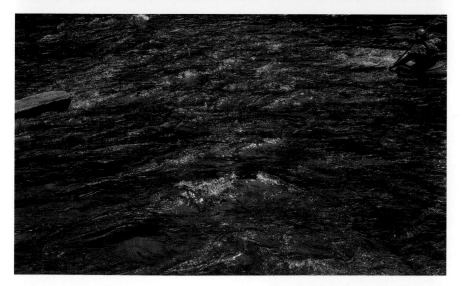

The paddler ferries into the eddy on the other side of the river.

S-Turn

The S-turn is a maneuver for crossing a chute or narrow current lane, or for traveling through a mid-river eddy, going in one side and out the other. It is actually a quick, truncated ferry—it begins with a peel-out and ends with an eddy turn, and it requires you to lean the boat first one way and then the other in quick succession.

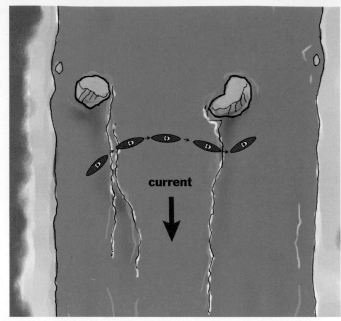

Think of the S-turn as a ferry for traveling short distances. It begins with a standard peel-out and ends with an eddy turn.

The S-turn begins with a set-up for a peel-out.

Hit the eddy line with good speed and the same angle you would use for a peel-out.

74

Lean the boat downstream as you cross the eddy line and do a forward stroke or sweep to keep the bow from turning too far downstream.

Midway across the current, do a sweep stroke on the downstream side of the boat, while at the same time shifting to an upstream lean to move into the destination eddy.

Use forward strokes on the upstream side to push the boat into the eddy.

Safe within the eddy.

Surfing

Because river waves, unlike ocean waves, are stationary, surfing on the river is a different game than riding an ocean breaker. You don't go anywhere on a river wave: the whole point is to put your boat in exactly the right spot so you slide down the upstream face of the wave and counteract the downstream force of the current on your hull. You hang there, suspended—it's an exhilarating feeling. It's also a good first move to learn if you're getting into playboating.

To start, find a small or medium wave that has an eddy next to it, and enter the eddy. Look for a depression at the point where the trough of the wave (the lowest part) meets the water: this is the spot to shoot for when getting on the wave. In general, planing-hull boats surf better on steeper waves, and displacement-hull boats are more suited to flatter waves. Either way, you may have to lean back slightly to keep the bow from plowing into the water as you surf.

Planing Hull

Because a planing-hull boat is too slow to get over the side of the wave from downstream, you need to start at a point in the eddy that is level with or upstream of the wave. You exit the eddy and approach the wave at a sharp angle—almost perpendicular to the current, if necessary. Once on the wave, you can turn the boat back upstream with a sweep stroke to establish yourself.

Use forward strokes to move toward the upstream face of the wave. (Powerful waves such as the one shown here tend to move back and forth a lot, which is why the paddler here appears to be approaching from downstream. Beginning surfers will want to seek out smaller waves.)

Here, a stern draw is used to turn the bow perpendicular to the wave.

Established on the wave.

Surfin'!

Displacement Hull

With a displacement-hull boat, you need to start downstream of the wave. Build up some speed, break through the eddy line, and cross over the side of the wave. Try to make your approach as perpendicular to the wave as possible—the displacement hull does not turn as easily as the planing hull, and you'll get pushed downstream if you have too much angle. A rudder works well for keeping yourself on the wave.

Use forward strokes to move toward the upstream face of the wave.

You sometimes will need to continue paddling until you are established on the wave.

Once your boat starts to settle onto the upstream face, use rudder strokes to stay perpendicular to the wave.

Riding the wave.

INTERNATIONAL SCALE OF RIVER DIFFICULTY

Developed by the organization American Whitewater , this rating system is a general guide to sections of rivers. Specific ratings are necessarily subjective and inexact, because aside from depth and flow, river features cannot be quantified. Classifications also may vary according to region and the opinion of the evaluators. Furthermore, rivers change character according to rainfall, storms, and dam releases, so rapids that are Class III one day may be Class V the next.

Use a rating as a guideline, but always check local conditions and get informed advice before attempting a new stretch.

Class I   Easy

Fast-moving water with riffles and small waves.
Few or no obstructions, all easy to avoid.
Risk to swimmers is slight.
Self-rescue is easy.

Class II   Novice

Straightforward rapids with wide, clear channels that are obvious without scouting.
Occasional maneuvering may be required, but rocks and medium-size waves are easily avoided by trained paddlers.
Swimmers are seldom injured, and group rescue, while helpful, is seldom needed.

Class III   Intermediate

Rapids with moderate, irregular waves that may be difficult to avoid and are capable of swamping an open canoe.
May include fast current and narrow passages that require complex maneuvers and good boat control.
Large waves, holes, and strainers may be present but are easily avoided.
Strong eddies and powerful current effects may be present, particularly on large-volume rivers.
Scouting is advisable for inexperienced parties.
Chance of injury while swimming is low, but group assistance may be needed to prevent long swims.

Class IV   Advanced

Intense, powerful rapids requiring precise boat handling in turbulent water.

Depending on the character of the river, there may be long, unavoidable waves and holes or constricted passages demanding fast maneuvers under pressure.

A fast, reliable eddy turn may be needed to navigate a drop, to pull over and scout rapids, or to rest.

Rapids may require "must make" moves above dangerous hazards.

Scouting is necessary the first time the stretch is run.

Risk of injury to swimmers is moderate to high, and water conditions may make rescue difficult.

Group assistance is often essential but requires practiced skills.

The ability to perform a strong Eskimo roll is highly recommended.

Class V   Expert

Extremely long, obstructed, or violent rapids that expose the paddler to above-average risk of injury.

Drops may contain very large, unavoidable waves and holes, or steep and congested chutes with complex, demanding routes.

Rapids often continue for long distances between pools or eddies, demanding a high level of fitness.

What eddies exist may be small, turbulent, or difficult to reach.

Several of the above factors may combine in the most difficult water of this class.

Scouting is mandatory.

Rescue extremely difficult, even for experts.

A very reliable Eskimo roll and above-average rescue skills are essential.

Class VI   Extreme

Features of Class V extended to the limits of navigability.

Nearly impossible and very dangerous.

Rescue may be impossible.

For teams of experts only, and only in favorable water levels after close study with all precautions.

The frequency with which a rapid is run should have no effect on this rating, as a number of Class VI rapids are regularly attempted.

7

Safety and Rescue

Running whitewater in a small boat is inherently dangerous. In fact, the danger is part of the appeal. But there is a line between a calculated risk and a foolish one, and the consequences of a bad decision are severe enough that you don't want to cross it.

Making a smart decision about whether or not to run a difficult stretch of river involves two basic questions: (1) Do you know what you're getting into? (2) Do you have the skills to get through it?

Answering the first question involves knowledge about the river that lies ahead. Answering the second question is a judgment call, and the right answer varies with the personality of the boater. Bold paddlers may be wise to talk themselves out of trying something they're not sure of, whereas the more timid may have to be nudged into it. Know thyself, but follow this general rule: Never talk yourself—or anyone else—into trying something dangerous if you or that other person lack the skills necessary to survive the possible outcome.

THE PADDLING GROUP

Beginners, especially, should paddle in a group that includes at least one experienced paddler.

In a downriver group, the lead boater should be a strong paddler who, ideally, knows the particular river. But even on unfamiliar water, a skilled boater can run a rapid, then get out and direct the trailing members of the group to the best route through. (See the Universal River Signals on the next page). The last boat in the group, the "sweep boat," should also have an experienced paddler, and this person must carry rescue gear and a first-aid kit and know how to use them. The least experienced or skilled paddlers should stay between the lead and sweep boats.

Five Factors Associated with Boating Fatalities

Statistics show five factors recur in boating fatalities.

1. Lack of PFD

At the scene of fatal boating accidents, PFDs are often found inside a swamped boat or floating beside it. Failure to have a PFD, or to wear it, is a common ingredient in drownings.

2. Cold Water or Air

Hypothermia caused by immersion in cold water is a leading cause of death in boating accidents. Such accidents often occur in the spring, when the air temperature is warm but the water is still cold, and boaters are not dressed warmly enough. Layered clothing of the right fabrics is essential in cold weather, especially when water is involved.

3. Inexperience

Inexperienced paddlers with no formal training are more likely to be victims of fatal accidents than trained, experienced paddlers.

4. Alcohol

Alcohol is a leading contributor to boating fatalities, as it inhibits both coordination and judgment.

5. Inability to Swim

Nonswimmers are more frequent drowning victims than swimmers.

Adapted from *The American Canoe Association's Canoe and Kayaking Instruction Manual* by Laurie Gullion. Used with permission of Menasha Ridge Press.

SCOUTING THE RIVER

When you're headed downriver and you approach a difficult-looking stretch, remember that you always have two choices: you can run it or carry around it. How can you possibly make this decision without seeing what's ahead? You can't. If you come to a blind corner, paddle to shore and get out of the boat to scout ahead. In a straight run, you can rarely see a whole stretch of river from down there at river level in your boat. If no one in your group has run the stretch, paddle to shore and walk downstream along the bank to scout it.

From a vantage point above the river, look at the whole rapid, from top to bottom, and visualize where you will enter and where you will exit. Can you locate the eddies and holes and plot a good route through the rapid? What are the hazards? Is there a way around them? If not, do you have the skills to navigate them?

At this point you have to soberly assess your own skills and how they match up with the challenges. Then answer this basic question: Are you ready for the consequences of running the stretch? If you can't avoid a big hole that's likely to flip you, do you have a solid Eskimo roll? Are you confident about doing a wet exit? Do you know what to do if someone throws you a rope?

Such decisions are complicated by the fact that whitewater kayakers, as a group, tend to be risk-takers, a personality profile that may include confidence, optimism, or simply a thrill-seeking defiance of danger. It's also true that most decisions about whitewater involve uncertainty. But in making such decisions, a veteran boater factors in the worst-case scenario and what he needs to do to survive it.

The very best way to orient yourself to the water is to bring someone who has paddled the route. Otherwise, talk to someone who has or consult guidebooks, maps, local paddling clubs, or paddling shops for river information. In using guidebooks, remember that river ratings are general guidelines that should be supported with more current and local information. You cannot assess the nature of a stretch solely on its difficulty rating. Fifty feet of Class III water is much less challenging than a full mile of it. Also, check the river level on the day of the run. Levels vary dramatically with rainfall, drought, or dam releases, and there is no way to know the state of a river on a particular day without checking.

Finally, if you'll be paddling several miles, check a map to see where roads are in relation to the river, in case you have to pull out and go for help in an emergency.

Emergency! Help!

Paddle, PFD, or helmet waved overhead. Three long
    blasts on a whistle.
Means: "Assist the signaler as quickly as possible."

Stop!

Arms held straight out to sides, flapped up and
    down, or paddle held horizontal overhead and
    pumped up and down.
Means: "Potential hazard ahead."
Pass on signal to other boats in the party and wait for
    the "all clear" signal before proceeding.

All Clear

Paddle, turned flat, or arm, raised in vertical bar
    above the head.
Means: "Come ahead." In the absence of other direc-
    tions, proceed down the center of the river.
To signal paddlers which side of the river to run to
    avoid rapids or an obstruction, tilt the vertical "all
    clear" toward the side of the river with the pre-
    ferred route. Never point toward the obstacle to be
    avoided.

Attention

A series of short chirps on the whistle.
Used when no emergency exists but where the need
    to communicate is obvious and necessary.
This signal should not be given casually—only when
    other forms of communication are not working.

Safety and Rescue

RESCUE PRIORITIES

Flips in moving water are often sudden and followed by a confusion of overturned boats, swimmers, and floating equipment. Though it's natural to go after the expensive kayak floating toward a falls or the dry bag holding your good camera, every paddler should have the following sequence of rescue priorities fixed in mind: People, Boats, Equipment.

Rescue the swimmer first. If he's in a non-threatening situation, go for the boat. Often they can be rescued together. But be prepared to abandon the boat if it's putting you in a dangerous position or if all your attention must be focused on the swimmer. Lastly, retrieve equipment.

SAFE SWIMMING POSITION

As a general rule, if you are thrown from a boat in fast water, immediately roll onto your back and float with your legs downstream, knees slightly bent and feet out of the water. This position lets you fend off rocks with your feet, rather than your head. Never stand up in fast water that is more than ankle-deep. The force of rushing water can shove a lifted foot between rocks so tightly that you can be knocked over and held under. Standing up in fast water is one of the most common causes of ankle and leg injuries—and worse, of drowning—among boaters.

There are three exceptions to the safe swimming position. (1) If you see a route to shore through navigable water, turn over on your stomach and swim aggressively toward it. In some situations, you can stay on your back and backstroke upstream into an eddy (just like back-ferrying in a boat). In any case, there are times when taking action is better than floating into a worse situation. (2) If you're being swept into a strainer—a downed tree or other obstruction with water flowing through it—turn around and approach it head-first. This position will let you pull yourself up onto the strainer with your arms. If you approach feet-first, the force of the current may drive you into the strainer below the surface and entrap you. (3) If you are about to be swept over a steep vertical drop, ball up: tuck your knees against your chest and wrap your arms around your legs.

STAYING WITH THE BOAT

If you're ejected from your boat and it is within reach, hang onto it— if you can do so without endangering yourself. Grab the upstream grab loop, and always stay upstream of the boat. If you're downstream of the boat in a strong current, the boat can push you against an obstruction and pin you there. Don't get caught between your boat and a rock, and always be ready to let go of the boat if it's dragging you into a dangerous situation—it can be replaced.

If you are ejected from your boat in fast water, it's usually best to enter the safe swimming position. Float through the rapids on your back with your knees bent and your feet facing downstream. The rule is: "Toes and nose on the surface."

It's sometimes advisable to abandon the safe swimming position and swim for shore if there's a route through relatively safe water, especially if you're about to be swept into a more dangerous situation downstream. In these instances, roll over on your stomach and swim aggressively for safety.

ROPE RESCUE

A basic rule of river ethics is that every paddler should be prepared to rescue himself or others. Rope throwing is an essential rescue technique for whitewater paddlers. Every kayak in a group should carry a throw bag and every paddler should be practiced in throwing one. Putting a throw bag where you want it takes a little practice. Before a whitewater trip, each member should spend some time tossing a throw bag at a target. You may get only one shot in a critical situation. If there is only one rope in your group, it should be in the most experienced paddler's boat.

Two general rules of rope rescue: (1) Never tie a rope to yourself, whether you're the thrower or the swimmer. You must be able to release the rope if it's pulling you under. (2) Carry a knife. Cutting a rope may save a life in the case of entanglement.

Rope-Thrower's Position

When your group approaches a difficult stretch where capsizing is likely, a rope-thrower should be positioned on shore at a spot just downstream of the stretch, one that has solid footing and from which the swimmer can be pulled into calm water or an eddy.

Throw

First yell to the swimmer to get his attention. Then pull a few feet of rope from the throw bag and hold it in your non-throwing hand. When you're ready to throw, yell "Rope!" and fling the bag toward the swimmer with an underhand or sidearm toss, holding the tag end of the rope with your non-throwing hand. The rope should land a little downstream of the swimmer, so he's floating toward, not away, from it. In other words, throw long, not short. The swimmer can always grab a rope that goes over him, but a short throw may be out of his reach.

The rope thrower should be downstream of the swimmer and should throw the rope when the swimmer is still upstream of him.

Throw the rope underhand, aimed over the swimmer or just downstream of him—never short or upstream. You can always pull in some rope if the throw is too long.

Bringing the Swimmer In

Once the swimmer grabs the rope, brace yourself for his weight by leaning back or sitting down and digging your heels into the ground. Hold on and let the current swing him into shore. Don't pull the rope out of his hands trying to yank him in.

Swimmer's Grip and Position

If you're being rescued, hold the thrown rope to your chest once you catch it—never tie or wrap it around any part of your body. Roll over on your back with the rope over your shoulder while being pulled in. If you face forward on your stomach, your face will get the full force of the water your head could be towed under.

REACH-THROW-ROW-TOW-GO

When a paddler goes overboard and you're faced with a rescue decision, remember this lifesaver's adage. The sequence proceeds from shore-based, to boat-based, to water-based rescue.

REACH. First try to reach the swimmer while standing on shore.

THROW. If you can't reach him, throw him a rope.

ROW AND TOW. If you have no rope or he's too far away to reach with a rope, paddle or row out to him and tow him in.

GO. The last resort is going into the water after a swimmer, which is the most dangerous option, especially for someone untrained in lifesaving.

Lie on your back with the rope over your shoulder when being towed to shore.

Wrong

If you are face-down when being towed, your head can be dragged underwater.

Anyone going on an extended paddling trip, especially through remote areas, should take a first aid course offered by the American Red Cross. A number of excellent first aid books are also available for reference.

Training in cardiopulmonary resuscitation (CPR) is strongly recommended for anyone who paddles frequently. Victims of near-drowning have been resuscitated even after extended periods (in at least one case, more than an hour) underwater.

The purpose of this section of the book is to familiarize you with the main medical problems associated with paddling.

HYPOTHERMIA

Hypothermia is the cooling of body temperature to 95 degrees Fahrenheit or lower by exposure to cold air or water. Moderate hypothermia can be debilitating, and a severe case can cause death. Since water conducts heat away from the body thirty-two times faster than air, immersion hypothermia is of particular concern to boaters. It can occur even when the air temperature is warm. A summer dunking in a cold stream or lake, coupled with wind, rain, or cool evening temperatures, can bring it on.

Uncontrolled shivering is the first sign that a person is becoming hypothermic. As his body temperature continues to drop, his speech may become slurred, his motor skills and coordination may be impaired, and his behavior become irrational. Suspect hypothermia if a person who has been cold for a while begins stumbling or acting strangely. In the final stages of hypothermia, when the body temperature drops below 90 degrees, shivering stops, and the victim is in grave danger.

The treatment for hypothermia is common sense: warm the victim. If his condition is from exposure to the air, add layers of clothes, get him out of the wind, and give him food and water. In severe cases, place him in a sleeping bag until help arrives.

A victim of immersion hypothermia—that brought on by immersion in cold water—should be removed from the water immediately and changed into dry clothes. Immersion hypothermia is a common contributing factor in drowning because it comes on fast and makes swimming and paddling difficult or impossible.

SHOULDER DISLOCATION

A shoulder dislocation is a painful and temporarily debilitating injury that occurs when the ball of the upper arm is knocked out of its socket. Paddlers are particularly vulnerable to this injury because their arms operate in a wide range of motion and are connected to a paddle that can be wrenched around by the force of water or jammed against a rock. Dislocations are more likely to occur when the arms rotate behind the body, or are held overhead or away from the body. Prevention, therefore, is largely a matter of good paddling technique: using body rotation rather than arm-reaching to perform strokes. Paddlers should also avoid reaching out or behind to fend off a rock with the paddle. With the upper arm away from the body, the force of the paddle hitting the rock can knock the arm out of its socket.

A dislocated shoulder can be slipped back into place on site by someone trained in the technique. Consult a wilderness first aid book. Otherwise, the arm should be placed in a sling and the victim taken to a doctor.

TENDINITIS

Tendinitis, another common paddling ailment, is an inflammation of the lining around the tendon that can be quite painful. It most commonly afflicts the forearms and the rotator cuff of the shoulder. Paddlers who take a long trip after a period of inactivity are most vulnerable. Stretching, exercise, and pre-trip training will reduce the chance of tendinitis. Treatment involves rest and anti-inflammatory drugs such as ibuprofen.

Safety and Rescue

Resources

BOOKS AND VIDEOS

Canoe & Kayak Techniques: Whitewater Kayaking,
    edited by Dave Harrison
    1998. Stackpole Books.
    A collection of short, incisive articles from *Canoe &*
    Kayak magazine on stroke technique, rolling, and
    river moves, with excellent illustrations by Bruce
    Morser.

Whitewater Paddling: Strokes and Concepts, by Eric
    Jackson
Playboating: Moves and Training, by Eric Jackson
    1998 and 2000. Stackpole Books.
    These two photo-rich volumes from freestyle
    champ Eric Jackson show the moves and techniques
    that made him famous. Especially of interest to
    playboaters who want to learn the cool moves.
    Great photos by Skip Brown.

The Bombproof Roll and Beyond, by Paul Dutky
    1993. Menasha Ridge Press.
    A classic text on rolling and edge control. Includes
    many types and variations of rolls for whitewater
    kayakers.

The Kayak Roll by Kent Ford
    2003. Performance Video.
    An extremely helpful instructional DVD by one
    of the leading kayak instructors and authors in
    the U.S.

River Rescue: A Manual for Whitewater Safety, 3rd ed., by
    Les Bechdel and Slim Ray
    1989. Appalachian Mountain Club.
    The definitive guide to river rescue.

MAGAZINES

Canoe & Kayak
10526 NE 68th Street, Suite 3
Kirkland, WA 98033
www.canoekayak.com

Paddler
PO Box 775450
Steamboat Springs, CO 80477
www.paddlermagazine.com

ORGANIZATIONS

American Canoe Association
7432 Alban Station Blvd., Suite B-232
Springfield, VA 22150
(703) 451-0141
www.acanet.org

American Rivers
1025 Vermont Ave NW, Suite 720
Washington, DC 20005
(202) 347-7550
www.amrivers.org

American Whitewater
1424 Fenwick Lane
Silver Spring, MD 20910
(866) 262-8429
www.americanwhitewater.org

SCHOOLS

Nantahala Outdoor Center
13077 Highway 19 West
Bryson City, NC 28713
www.noc.com

Rocky Mountain Outdoor Center
228 North F Street
Salida, CO 81201
(800) 255-5784
www.rmoc.com

Zoar Outdoor
7 Main Street
PO Box 245
Charlemont, MA 01339
(800) 532-7483
www.kayaklesson.com

MANUFACTURERS

The companies below carry full lines of kayaks or paddles in a range of styles and prices. For a more extensive
list, check the annual buyer's guide issues of *Paddler*
and *Canoe & Kayak* magazines.

Carlisle Paddles
PO Box 488
4562 North Down River Road
Grayling, MI 49738
(989) 348-9886
www.carlislepaddles.com

Dagger
111 Kayaker Way
Easley, SC 29642
(800) 433-1969
www.dagger.com

Liquidlogic
765 Crest Road
Flat Rock, NC 28731
(828) 698-5778
www.liquidlogickayaks.com

Wave Sport
3761 Old Glenola Rd.
Trinity, NC 27370
www.wavesport.com

Werner Paddles, Inc.
33415 SR 2
Sultan, WA 98294
(800) 275-3311
www.wernerpaddles.com